Anonymous

Translation of the Law of Railroads for the Island of Cuba

Anonymous

Translation of the Law of Railroads for the Island of Cuba

ISBN/EAN: 9783744696470

Printed in Europe, USA, Canada, Australia, Japan

Cover: Foto ©ninafisch / pixelio.de

More available books at **www.hansebooks.com**

TRANSLATION

OF THE

LAW OF RAILROADS

FOR THE

ISLAND OF CUBA,

AND

REGULATIONS FOR ITS EXECUTION,

WITH ADDITIONS TO DATE.

(1895.)

DIVISION OF CUSTOMS AND INSULAR AFFAIRS,
WAR DEPARTMENT
JULY, 1899,

WASHINGTON:
GOVERNMENT PRINTING OFFICE.
1899.

The Colonial Department, under date of September 27 last, and under No. 1678, communicates to His Excellency the Governor-General, the following Royal Order:

YOUR EXCELLENCY: In view of the necessity to clearly establish the legislation in force in that Island with regard to Railroads in order to avoid the doubts which appear in the questions submitted by the General Inspection of Public Works, and which also appear in the proceedings which take place in that Island with relation to concessions of this class of roads of communication;

Whereas, after the Budget Law of June 5, 1880, was promulgated, there were declared as preferred lines those mentioned therein, the concession of which the Government was authorized to grant, declaring the two General Laws of November 23, 1877, and their corresponding Regulations, applicable in so far as they do not conflict with the prescriptions of the said law;

Whereas the law of November 23, 1877, prescribed all the rules necessary for the concessions to construct Railroads of general interest and those of private use and tramways, and which in its article 80 establishes that the laws, decrees, and other provisions issued prior thereto which conflict with the same are repealed;

Whereas the Decree-law of November 14, 1868, on new general bases for the legislation on Public Works has been repealed in so far as it refers to Railroads, from the time the special Railroad Law was promulgated and declared applicable to the one of that Island;

Whereas for the proper application of the said Railroad Law and the Regulations for its observance it is necessary to make in its text those alterations necessary to apply the same to the administrative organization of that province, this should not be an obstacle for the immediate application of its prescriptions as ordered by the law of June 5, 1880, consulting any doubts which may arise in so doing;

His Majesty the King (whom God preserve) has deemed it proper to state to Your Excellency that the legislation in force for the concession, construction, and operation of Railroads of that Island is that which was expressly ordered to be observed by article 27 of the Budget Law of June 5, 1880, or contained in the General Laws of November 23, 1877, and their corresponding Regulations, in so far as they do not conflict with the prescriptions established by said law, said legislation having repealed all prior measures issued in conflict with the same. This I communicate to Your Excellency by Royal Order for your information and consequent effects.

And His Excellency having ordered its compliance under date of October 18, last, it is published in the *Gaceta*, for general information. Habana, November 24, 1882.

M. DIAZ DE LA QUINTANA,
Secretary of the General Government.

(*Gaceta* of December 3.)

3

The General Law of Railroads, and the Law for the police of the same, of November 23, 1877, and the Regulations for its application of May 24, 1878, now in force in the Peninsula, having been extended to this Island, I have ordered their publication in the *Gaceta*, for general information.

M. DIAZ DE LA QUINTANA,
Secretary of the General Government.

Habana, January 5, 1883.

LAWS.

Don Alfonso XII, by the Grace of God, Constitutional King of Spain: Know all ye who see and understand these presents: That in accordance with the bases approved by the Cortes which were promulgated as a law on December 29, 1876, making use of the authorization granted by the same law to my Secretary of Public Works, hearing the Secretary of the Navy in the matters of his special competence, and hearing also the full Council of State and the Consulting Board of Roads, Canals, and Ports, and in conformity with my Council of Secretaries, I have decreed and sanctioned the following law:

CHAPTER I.

CLASSIFICATION OF RAILROADS.

ARTICLE 1. This law refers to all railroads, whatever be the system of traction employed.

ART. 2. Railroads are divided into lines of general service and of private service.

ART. 3. Railroads of general service are those devoted to public operation for transportation of passengers and traffic of merchandise; those of private service are devoted to the exclusive operation of a given industry or to private use.

ART. 4. The lines constructed and those included in the law of July 2, 1870, their branch and special lines, form the general plan of railroads for the purposes of this law, all of which are mentioned here, as follows:

Northern System.—Madrid to Valladolid, Valladolid to Burgos, Burgos to Irún, San Isidro de Dueñas (Venta de Baños) to Alar del Rey, Alar del Rey to Santander, Quintanilla de las Torres to Orbó, Madrid to Valladolid by Segovia. From the line from Madrid to Valladolid to Segovia. Medina del Campo to Zamora. Medina del Campo to Salamanca, Tudela (Castejón) to Bilbao. Minas de Triano to the Ria de Bilbao.

Northeastern system and its junction with the Northern.—Madrid to Zaragoza. Zaragoza to Alsasua. Zaragoza to Barcelona. Barcelona to Granollers. Granollers to Rambla de Sta. Coloma de Farnés. Barcelona to Mataró. Mataró to Arenys de Mar. Arenys de Mar to Rambla de Sta. Coloma. Rambla de Sta. Coloma to Gerona. Gerona to Figueras. Figueras to the frontier of France. To France by the Central Pyrenees. Tardienta to Huesca. Tarragona to Martorell. Martorell to Barcelona. Lérida to Montblanch. Montblanch to Reus. Reus to Tarragona. Barcelona to Sarriá. Selgua to Barbastro. Granollers to San Juan de las Abadesas. Mollet to Caldas de Montbuy. Manresa to Guardiola by Berga. Minas de Montsech to the French frontier by the Valley of Arán. Alcocer to Valls. Valls by Villanueva y Geltrú to Barcelona. Lérida to Puente del Rey. Zaragoza to Escatrón. Val de Zafan to Gargallo. Val de Zafan to Alcañiz, Reus, and Tarragona. Val de Zafan to Utrillas by Gargallo and Andorra. Utrillas to la Zaida. Valladolid to Calatayud. Segovia to the line from Valladolid to Calatayud. Baides to Soria and Castejón.

Eastern system and its junction with the Northeastern.—Madrid to Almansa. Almansa to Alicante. Almansa to Játiva. Albacete to Cartagena. Castillejo to Toledo. Aranjuez or Madrid to Cuenca. Alcázar de San Juan to Quintanar de la Orden. Játiva to Grao de Valencia. Valencia to Tarragona. *Cargagente to Gandia and Gandia to Denia* (animal traction). Cuenca to Henarejos. Cuenca to Valencia by Landete, and from this point to Teruel. Teruel to Gargallo by the River Alfambra and Utrillas. Teruel to Sagunto. Calatayud to Teruel and Lugo to Utrillas. Alicante to Murcia and its branches to Novelda and Torrevieja.

Southern system and its junction with the Eastern.—Madrid to Ciudad-Real (direct line). Alcazar de San Juan to Ciudad-Real. Manzanares to Córdoba. Córdoba to Sevilla. Sevilla to Jerez. Jerez to Trocadero. Puerto Real to Cadiz. Córdoba to Málaga. Córdoba to Belmez. Utrera to Morón. Utrera (junction) to Osuna. Campillos (Bobadilla) to Granada. Tharsis to Odiel River. Buitrón to the river of San Juan del Puerto. Buitrón to the line of Mérida to Sevilla. Sevilla to Huelva. Tharsis by Paimogo to the line of Beja. Mengibar to Jaén and Granada. Linares to Almeria. Murcia to Granada by Lorca. Vadollano to Linares and los Salidos. Osuna by Casariche. Jerez de la Frontera to Bonanza by Sanlucar. Cadiz to Campamento. Campamento to Málaga. Puente Genil to Linares. Zafra to Huelva.

Eastern system and its junction with the Southern and the Northern.—Ciudad-Real to Badajoz. Medellin to Miajadas. Belmez to Castillo de Almorchón. Madrid to Malpartida de Plasencia. Malpartida de Plasencia to Monfortinho. Talavera to Almorchón. Mérida to Sevilla. Mérida to Malpartida de Plasencia by Cáceres. Malpartida de Plasencia to Salamanca. Cáceres to the frontier of Portugal. Salamanca to the frontier of Portugal.

Northwestern system and its junction with the Northern.—Palencia to Ponferrada. Ponferrada to Coruña. Monforte to Orense. Orense to Vigo. Lugo to Rivadeo. Ferrol to Betanzos. Santiago to the port of Carril. Redondela to Marín by Pontevedra. León to Gijón. Sama de Langreo to Gijón. Sabero to El Burgo. Oviedo to Pravia by Trubia. Villabona to San Juan de Nieva. Zamora to Astorga by Benavente.

Balearic Islands.—Palma to Alcudia and Santa Maria or Manacor. Branches to coal mines or mining districts and importing industrial centers.

ART. 5. All the lines included in the plan adopted by the previous article, and also those which may be included in the future in said plan are lines of general service. Lines devoted to the operation of coal veins and mines of importance may also be included in those of general service, when so classified.

ART. 6. The plan of railroads can not be changed or modified except by virtue of a law.

ART. 7. All the railroad lines of general service are of public ownership, and shall be considered as works of public utility, which are entitled to the right of eminent domain.

ART. 8. The declaration that a railroad devoted to the operation of a coal vein or of mines of importance is of general service shall be made by a law. In order to obtain said declaration, a report of experts as to the importance of the mines shall in all cases be necessary. The report shall be made by the Secretary of Public Works after hearing the Superior Consulting Board of Mines.

CHAPTER II.

CONCESSION AND AUTHORIZATION TO CONSTRUCT RAILROADS OF GENERAL SERVICE.

ART. 9. The construction of lines of general service may be undertaken by the Government, by companies, or by individuals.

ART. 10. In order that the Government may undertake the construction of a line with national funds, or with the aid of the provinces or towns, it is necessary that the line be included in the plan, and, besides, its immediate execution must be authorized by a special law.

ART. 11. When a line of general service is to be constructed by individuals or companies, the concession must always be preceded by a law fixing the conditions under which the concession is to be granted.

ART. 12. The construction of lines of general service may be aided with public funds:

1. By carrying on certain works.

2. By delivering to the companies at stated periods a part of the capital invested.

3. By allowing the use of works constructed for public use compatible with the use of the railroads.

4. By granting exemption from customs duties upon the material of construction and operation of the railroads, complying strictly with the provisions of the laws of the Budget or any others in force.

ART. 13. The provinces and towns directly interested in the construction of a line of general service shall contribute with the State to the subsidy granted in the proportion and manner prescribed by the law referred to in Article 11.

ART. 14. The aid which is to be given the constructing companies, once determined by the Laws of Concession, the concession shall be offered at public auction, under the terms fixed, for three months, and shall be awarded to the highest bidder, with the obligation to pay to the proper party the cost of the plans of the project, which may have served as a basis for the concession; the said cost shall be fixed before making the public sale in the cases and in the form determined by the Regulations.

ART. 15. In order to be able to bid at the auctions, it must be shown that 1 per cent of the total value of the railroad, according to the approved estimate, has been deposited as a guaranty of the proposals which are submitted.

ART. 16. In no case shall the concession titles to lines of general service be issued until the holder of the concession shows that he has deposited, as a guaranty of his obligations, 5 per cent of the amount of the estimate if the concession has a subsidy, and 3 per cent if there be none.

If the holder of the concession allows fifteen days to pass without making the deposit, the award shall be declared null, with the forfeiture of the bond given, and the concession of the line shall be again offered at auction within the period of forty days.

ART. 17. The companies holding concessions of lines enjoying subsidies can not dispose of the amounts deposited as a guaranty of the construction of the railroad, until they have totally finished the works which are the objects of the concession. In case the line has no subsidy, the guaranty may be returned when it is proven that there are works finished equivalent to a third of the cost of the works included in the concession. The said completed works shall remain as a guaranty for the fulfillment of the conditions stipulated.

ART. 18. The project which may have served as a basis for the concession of a line can not be changed in any manner whatsoever by the holder of the concession, without first obtaining the proper authorization from the Secretary of Public Works, granted with the requisites prescribed by the Regulations of the present Law.

ART. 19. When, as a consequence of the changes referred to in the preceding article, the cost of the work is diminished, the direct subsidy shall be diminished in proportion to such diminution; if the changes or modifications increase the cost of the work, even when these changes perfect the same, and advantages accrue by its use, the subsidy granted by the Law of Concession shall never be increased thereby.

ART. 20. When the work is completed and the operation of the line belongs to the owner of the concession, the State shall reserve to itself the supervision thereof, through its expert agents, so that the operation of the line may be conducted according to the conditions stipulated.

ART. 21. The concessionnaire may, after proper authorization from the Secretary of Public Works, transfer his rights, and the person acquiring them shall remain obligated under the same conditions and with the same guaranties to the fulfillment of the stipulated conditions.

ART. 22. The concessions of lines of general service shall be granted, at the most, for ninety-nine years.

ART. 23. At the expiration of the period of the concession the State shall acquire the granted line with all its dependencies, and shall fully enjoy the right of operation.

ART. 24. No railroad concession shall create a monopoly in favor of companies, or individuals, and no other subsequent concessions for roads, canals, railroads, works of navigation, or others, in the same district where the railroad is situated, or in another adjoining it or distant therefrom, shall serve as a basis for claiming any indemnity whatsoever in favor of any of the owners of the concessions.

CHAPTER III.

FORMALITIES WITH WHICH THE AUTHORIZATION OR CONCESSION SHALL BE REQUESTED.

ART. 25. When the Government shall deem it proper to construct with public funds one of the railroad lines included in the plan, it shall submit to the Cortes, together with the form of authorization, the following documents:

1. A memorial descriptive of the plan.

2. A general plan and longitudinal profile.

3. An estimate of the cost of construction and the annual cost of repairs and maintenance of the work.

4. An estimate of the material necessary for the operation and the annual cost of its repair and maintenance.

5. A schedule of the highest rates to be demanded for fares and transportation.

6. Such other conditions as may be deemed proper.

ART. 26. Individuals and companies who may desire the concession of a railroad line declared to be of general service, shall address their petition to the Secretary of Public Works, and must present with it the documents constituting the plan, and must also show that there has been deposited as a guaranty of the plan 1 per cent of the total cost of the works and the material for the operation of the line, according to the estimates.

ART. 27. The plan being approved and the conditions of the concessions being mutually accepted, the Government shall present to the Cortes the proper form of Law, with the document mentioned in Article 25.

ART. 28. When individuals or companies desire a declaration that the railroad line they propose to construct is of public service, they shall address their petition to the Secretary of Public Works, together with a memorial and a general plan and profile of the line. The said Secretary shall then give a hearing, at which the Provincial Deputations and the Municipal Corporations interested in the construction may be heard, as well as the corporations and authorities which, in their judgment, may shed light on the subject, as well as the Consulting Board of Roads, Canals, and Ports; and he shall then submit, as a result of this hearing, the form of Law to the Cortes in order that the railroad be included in the plan of those of general service. This declaration being made, the proceedings determined by the articles of Chapter III to grant the concession, if there be grounds for it, shall be followed.

ART. 29. When two or more petitions are presented with different plans, so that a railroad of public service is declared of general utility, a hearing on all of the plans, as provided for by the previous article, shall be given, so that the law making the declaration shall redound to the benefit of the one offering greater advantages to the general interests of the country.

CHAPTER IV.

PRIVILEGES AND GENERAL EXEMPTIONS GRANTED TO COMPANIES HOLDING CONCESSIONS OF RAILROADS OF GENERAL UTILITY.

ART. 30. Foreign capital employed in the construction of railroads, and loans for this purpose, shall be under the protection of the State, and are exempt from reprisals, confiscations, or attachments by reason of war.

ART. 31. The following shall be granted to all railroad companies of general utility:

1. The public lands which the road and its appurtenances may have to occupy.

2. The rights which the inhabitants of the districts through which the line passes have to cut timber, to pasturage, and other rights, shall be enjoyed by the employees and laborers of the companies, and for the care of its draft animals employed in the works.

3. The right to open quarries, gather loose stone, construct lime, chalk, and brick kilns, to deposit materials and to establish workshops on lands adjoining the lines. If these be public lands, the right shall be used after giving previous notice to the local authority; but if they be private property, or property of the province or municipalities, the lands may be used only after the parties have agreed, either by mutual consent or by virtue of the law of eminent domain, with reference to the temporary occupation.

4. The exclusive right to collect, while the concession lasts and according to the schedule of rates approved, the rates charged for passengers and freight, without prejudice to those belonging to other companies.

5. For the lines which can revert to the State, the exemption from the mortgage charges due on account of the charges for transfers of property, made by the construction of these railroad lines and their appurtenances, by virtue of the law of eminent domain, as well as those arising from contracts for the same purposes, made by the companies with individuals.

CHAPTER V.

FORFEITURE OF THE CONCESSION OF RAILROADS OF GENERAL SERVICE.

ART. 32. The declaration of the forfeiture of the concession of a line of general service shall always be made after proceedings instituted in accordance with the Regulations.

ART. 33. In order to declare the forfeiture of a concession the full council of State must be heard.

ART. 34. The holder of the concession may appeal from the decision of the Government, declaring the forfeiture to the administrative officers where these matters are in controversy within the period of two months from the day of publication in the Official Gazette.

If he does not appeal within this time the ministerial decision shall be considered as consented to, and there shall be no recourse whatever against it.

ART. 35. The forfeiture of a concession on account of failure to perform, attributed to the holder thereof, shall always be accompanied by the loss of the bond to the benefit of the State.

ART. 36. The concessions of railroads included in this chapter shall lapse in any of the following cases:

1. If the works are not commenced or finished within the time fixed by the law of concession, except in cases of force majeure, so declared after proceedings, in which the full Council of State shall be heard. When any of these cases occur, and are duly proven, the time prescribed by the Secretary of Public Works may be extended for the period absolutely necessary, which can never exceed that fixed in the concession for the construction of the works. The extension having ended, the concession shall lapse if the provisions prescribed at the time of its execution are not fulfilled.

2. If the public service of the line be totally or partially interrupted, except in cases of force majeure, declared to be such in the manner prescribed by the first paragraph of this article.

3. When the company owning the concession is dissolved by an administrative or judicial act, or declared in bankruptcy.

ART. 37. In the cases of forfeiture by dissolution or bankruptcy, the Secretary of Public Works shall take possession of the works and of the fixed and rolling stock, taking charge of the operation through a council which he shall appoint, in which he shall give representation to the stock and bond holders and to the creditors of the lapsed company.

Art. 38. If, when the forfeiture is declared, the works have not been begun, the administration shall be freed from all liability to the holder of the concession. If any of the works had been executed, or all of them, they shall be sold at auction, awarding the concession to the best bidder. The new owner of the concession shall then pay the former owner the amount offered at the auction.

The basis for this auction shall be the amount, according to appraisal, of the cost of the plan, the land purchased, the works executed, and the construction and operation material on hand, deducting the payments made to the concessionaire and delivered to the same in land, works, specie, etc. The appraisal shall be made by the Engineers of Roads, Canals, and Ports, whom the Secretary of Public Works may select, and by the experts appointed by the concessionaire.

Art. 39. If no bidder appears at the auction mentioned in the preceding article, a new auction shall be advertised during the period of two months, and with the basis of two-thirds of the amount of the appraisal. If no bidders appear at this new auction, a third and last auction shall be advertised during the period of one month, without any fixed basis.

Art. 40. If at any of the three auctions referred to in the preceding articles bids were made within the advertised conditions, the railroad shall be awarded to the best bidder, who shall pay as a guaranty the amount of 3 or 5 per cent of the value of the works, to be executed in accordance with the concession; and the effects of this law shall be applicable to the new concessionaire, the same as they were applicable to the former, and he shall be liable to all the provisions, substituting the former concessionaire in all his liabilities and rights.

Art. 41. From the cost of the works auctioned, which the bidder shall pay, as provided for by the previous article, the expenses of appraisal and auction shall be deducted, and the remainder shall be delivered to whom it may rightfully belong.

Art. 42. In case the concession is not awarded in any of the three consecutive auctions, the State shall take possession of the works, to continue them if it was considered convenient in accordance with the provisions of the law, without the original holder of the concession having the right to any indemnity whatsoever.

Chapter VI.

CONDITIONS OF CONSTRUCTION TO WHICH THAT OF RAILROADS FOR GENERAL SERVICE MUST CONFORM.

Art. 43. The railroads of general service shall be constructed according to the following conditions:

1. The gauge of the track or distance between the two interior sides of the rails shall be 1 meter 67 centimeters (6 Castilian feet).

2. The gauge of the tracks shall be 1 meter and 80 centimeters (6 feet 6 inches Castilian measurement).

3. The other dimensions, as well as the other conditions of construction, shall be fixed in each particular case by the Secretary of Public Works after hearing the Consulting Board of Roads, Canals, and Ports.

4. The roads of general service may be constructed with one or two tracks or by combining these systems.

ART. 44. When lines not included in the general system are to be established the technical conditions mentioned in the preceding article may be modified, and those to which the line must conform shall be fixed in a special law, which must precede the concession.

CHAPTER VII.

OPERATION OF RAILROADS.

ART. 45. Every railroad shall have two distinct uses—for passengers and for freight.

ART. 46. The charges for each shall be fixed by the schedules of rates in force for each line.

ART. 47. The document of conditions of the concession shall designate the special schedule of rates for certain services to the State as well as those which are free. Among the latter is the carrying of the regular mails, which, as well as everything necessary for the operation of railroads, shall be determined by the Secretary of Public Works, with the concurrence of the proper Secretaries, as the case may be.

ART. 48. From the carrying companies and from individuals who use their own materials the legal freight only may be demanded.

ART. 49. After the first five years that the railroad is in operation, and thereafter every five years, a revision of the schedules of rates shall be made.

If the Government, without injury to the interests of the company, believes that the rates may be lowered, but the company does not agree to the reduction, it may, nevertheless, be made by a law, guaranteeing to the company the total earnings of the last year and, besides, the average progressive increase of the earnings which they may have had in the last five years.

ART. 50. The companies may at any time reduce the schedule of rates as they may deem best, advising the Secretary of Public Works.

ART. 51. When schedules of rates are to be changed it shall be duly announced beforehand to the public.

ART. 52. There shall be established along the roads a telegraph line, the number of wires of which, and other conditions as to the general and official service, shall be determined in the document of conditions of the concession.

ART. 53. When the public service of the company is totally or partially interrupted owing to its own fault, the Government shall, as a matter of course, take the steps necessary to secure said public service temporarily at the expense of the company.

Within a period of six months the company holding the concession must prove that it has sufficient means to continue its operation; the company may cede the operation to another company or third person, after a previous special authorization of the Government,

If even by this proceeding the service is not renewed the concession shall be considered as forfeited and, therefore, what is prescribed by the articles of Chapter V shall be complied with.

ART. 54. The operation of railroads belonging to the State shall be carried on by the Government or by companies which may contract for the service at public auction, as it may be best for the interests of the public.

ART. 55. In all concessions there shall be stated the right of the Government to the necessary supervision and intervention, so as to keep the service of the railroad in good condition and to secure the expenses and receipts of the company.

ART. 56. In the Law and Regulations to be made for the police of railroads there shall be determined whatever is proper for their maintenance and security.

CHAPTER VIII.

PLANS FOR RAILROAD LINES.

ART. 57. The Secretary of Public Works shall order that plans of the lines included in the general system be made, or those begun be completed, by Engineers of Roads, Canals, and Ports, so that with the respective plans of the lines the Government may submit to the Cortes the proper form of law authorizing the auction.

ART. 58. The Secretary of Public Works may authorize individuals or companies to make plans so as to collect the facts and documents which, according to the provisions of this Law, are necessary to obtain the concession of a line. This authorization can not be understood as granting any right whatever against the State, nor limiting in any way the right which the Department of Public Works has to grant equal authorizations to those who may want to study the same line.

ART. 59. The concession for plans shall be preceded by the deposit of the bond, that the Secretary of Public Works shall consider sufficient, to answer for the damages which the said study may occasion in the lands traversed by the line.

The approval of the plans shall not take place until it has been gone over on the ground by the Engineers of the State and the opinion given by the Consulting Board of Roads, Canals, and Ports.

CHAPTER IX.

INTERVENTION OF THE GOVERNMENT IN RAILROADS.

ART. 60. The Secretary of Public Works shall decide all questions regarding the construction and operation of railroads, as well as the police of the same, and the compliance with the document of conditions, including the schedules of rates for storage, loading and unloading, and transportation.

ART. 61. The supervision as to the maintenance and operation of the railroads appertaining to the Government shall be made through the Secretary of Public Works.

The Regulations and special instructions which may be ordered for the fulfillment of this law shall determine the organization of the personnel devoted to this service, the conditions of efficiency which the individuals of the said service must show when they are not experts of Public Works, and the duties of both.

CHAPTER X.

RAILROADS DEVOTED TO PRIVATE USE.

ART. 62. Railroads devoted to the operation of an industry or to private use may be constructed without any other restrictions than those imposed by the Regulations as to safety and public health, provided that the works do not occupy or affect public property nor that there be required for their construction the exercise of the right of eminent domain.

ART. 63. The right to seize by eminent domain can not be granted to a railroad included in the preceding article, nor the occupation of State lands; but public lands may be seized and occupied in conformity with the General Law of Public Works.

ART. 64. When railroads devoted to the operation of an industry or to private use are of such importance that they are capable of rendering public service, the occupation of lands belonging to the State may be granted by means of a Law and the right of eminent domain.

ART. 65. After the concession to which the preceding articles refer has been made, the individual or company obtaining it may construct the railroad and use it as he or it may deem best, with no further intervention on the part of the Government than that relating to conditions of safety, police, and good government of property belonging to the public.

ART. 66. The individuals or companies who desire to construct and operate a railroad of those included in the preceding articles, shall address their petition to the Secretary of Public Works, accompanied by the plans.

ART. 67. The Secretary of Public Works, for his information, shall request all the reports which he may deem proper, the previous opinion of the Consulting Board of the Corps of Engineers of Roads, Canals, and Ports being an indispensable requisite.

ART. 68. These railroads, unless otherwise provided for in a special Law, shall be granted by the Government for ninety-nine years, whenever the occupation of public property is asked for.

When the railroads ask for the declaration of public utility, it shall be the subject of a law.

CHAPTER XI.

TRAMWAYS.

ART. 69. Under the name of tramways are designated, for the purposes of this law, the railroads constructed on the public highways.

ART. 70. The approval of the plans of tramways which are to occupy the roads belonging to the State or Province belongs to the Secretary of Public Works.

The Secretary of Public Works shall also approve, after proper proceedings in accordance with the Provincial and Municipal Law, the plans of tramways, the development of which demands the simultaneous occupation of roads belonging to the State or to the Province and of Municipal roads or the streets of towns.

ART. 71. When the tramways are to be constructed on municipal roads, the approval of the plans shall belong to the Civil Governors, who, in order to grant it, must hear the Engineers in Chief of Roads of the Provinces.

ART. 72. In all cases when the power to be used is other than animal force, the approval of the plans of the tramways belongs to the Secretary of Public Works.

ART. 73. The concession of tramways belongs to the Secretary of Public Works, when the works are to occupy State highroads of two or more Provinces, or shall simultaneously traverse highroads of the State and highways of the Provinces and of Municipalities, after proper proceedings, in accordance with the Provincial and Municipal laws in the last two cases.

ART. 74. When the tramways are to be constructed on highroads which are exclusively in charge of one Province, or traversing two or more Municipalities, the concession belongs to the Provincial Deputation.

ART. 75. The concessions belong to the Municipal Council when the tramways occupy roads which are in charge of a single Municipality. When they are essentially town roads, it must be preceded by the approval of the Interior Department.

ART. 76. Tramway concessions can not be granted for more than sixty years, and shall be subject to an auction in regard to the maximum schedule of rates or to the duration of the concession.

ART. 77. In the Regulations which shall be drawn for the compliance of the present law, the general conditions to which tramways must conform in relation to the technical conditions, as well as to the steps to be taken in the granting of the concession, shall be stated.

ART. 78. In the document of special conditions, which must form part of the concession of every tramway, the special conditions shall be determined which, besides the general ones to which the previous article refers, are to govern in matters of construction and operation.

GENERAL PROVISIONS.

ART. 79. The provisions of the present law shall not invalidate any of the rights acquired previously to its publication and in compliance with the then existing legislation.

ART. 80. All laws, decrees, and other provisions previously existing, which are in opposition to the present law, are hereby repealed.

Therefore, we command all Tribunals, Justices, Chiefs, Governors, and all other authorities, civil, military, and ecclesiastical, of any class and dignity whatsoever, to observe and to see that the present law is observed, carried out, and executed in all its parts.

Given at the Palace on the 23d of November, 1877.

I, THE KING.

C. FRANCISCO QUEIPO DE LLANO,
Secretary of Public Works.

LAW.

Don Alfonso XII, by the Grace of God Constitutional King of Spain.

Know all ye who see and understand these presents: That in accordance with the bases approved by the Cortes which were promulgated as a law on December 29, 1876; making use of the authorization granted by the same law to my Secretary of Public Works; hearing the Secretary of the Navy in the matters of his special competence, and hearing also the full Council of State and the Consulting Board of Roads, Canals, and Ports, and in conformity with my Council of Secretaries,

I have decreed and sanctioned the following law·

TITLE I.

PROVISIONS FOR THE PRESERVATION OF PUBLIC ROADS APPLICABLE TO RAILROADS.

ARTICLE 1. The Laws and Regulations of the Administration as to highways are applicable to Railroads when their object is—

1. The preservation of trenches, drains, walls, buildings, and other kinds of works.

2. The rights (*servitudes*) for the preservation of the roads charged on the adjoining cultivated lands.

3. The *servitudes* on these same lands as to laying out lines, constructions of all kinds, opening of ditches, free course of water, planting, pruning of trees, working of mines, lands, places for dumping refuse ore, quarries, and any other whatsoever. The zone to which these rights extend is 20 meters on each side of the railroad.

4. The prohibitions the object of which is to prevent all kinds of damage to the road.

5. Prohibiting the placing of hanging or projecting objects which may inconvenience or endanger persons on the road.

6. Prohibiting the establishment of deposits of materials, stones, earth, manure, products, or any other thing which may impede free transit.

TITLE II.

PROVISIONS FOR THE PRESERVATION OF ROADS WHICH REFER ESPECIALLY TO RAILROADS.

ART. 2. Along the whole distance of the railroad neither the entry nor the grazing of cattle shall be allowed. If the railroad has to cross a highway where cattle pass, the railroad shall always cross without changing or stopping the progress of the trains and in the manner provided for as a general rule for that crossing.

ART. 3. In the future, in a zone of 3 meters on each side of the railroad, only fencing walls shall be constructed, but no façades having openings or projections. This provision does not refer to buildings constructed before the promulgation of this law or the construction of a railroad, which may be separated and maintained in the condition in which they are, but can not be rebuilt. If it be necessary to demolish or change a building for the benefit of a railroad, the proceedings shall be according to the provisions of Article 11 of this Law.

ART. 4. Within the zone indicated in paragraph 3 of Article 1 no buildings may be constructed covered with thatch or other combustible materials when the railroad is operated by means of locomotives.

ART. 5. The prohibition to establish deposits of materials, earth, stones, or anything mentioned in the sixth paragraph of Article 1, in the case of railroads, includes 5 meters on each side of the road as to objects not inflammable and 20 meters as to inflammable objects.

ART. 6. The prohibition of the preceding article shall not be operative when—

1. The deposits of incombustible material shall not be higher than the road, when the latter is on an embankment.

2. The deposits of materials to be employed for fertilizing and cultivating lands, and harvests during their gathering, are temporary; but in case of fire due to the passing of locomotives the owners shall have no right to an indemnity.

ART. 7. The Governor of the Province may authorize, after hearing the Engineers of the Government and of the Companies, the deposit of uninflammable materials; but the authorization shall be revocable at his will. The Governor may not authorize deposits of inflammable materials.

ART. 8. The railroads throughout their length shall be fenced on both sides. The Secretary of Public Works, after hearing the Company, in case there be one, shall determine for each line the manner in which and time when the fencing is to be made. When railroads cross others on the same level, gates shall be constructed which shall be closed, and only opened when vehicles and cattle cross, as provided for in the regulations.

TITLE III.

PROVISIONS AS TO THE PRECEDING TITLES.

ART. 9. The distance fixed in paragraph 3 of Article 1 and in Articles 3 and 5 of this Law shall be measured from the lower line of the walls of the embankment of railroads, from the upper line of the clearing, and from the outer border of the trenches. If there be no such lines, the measures shall be from a line drawn a meter and a half from the outside of the railroad. The Regulations will fix the minimum distance from the stations at which buildings may be constructed or deposits established.

ART. 10. The Secretary of Public Works, in special cases, may reduce the distances to which the preceding article refers, after the proper steps are taken showing the necessity or convenience of the reduction, and if no harm is done to the regularity, preservation, and free transit of the road.

ART. 11. Whenever there exist individual rights previous to the construction of a railroad or the publication of this law, which rights can not be enforced, or if it be necessary to abolish these rights on account of the necessity or utility of the railroads, the rules established in the Law of July 17, 1836, shall be observed as to forcible condemnation by reason of public utility, and also the provisions of the Laws of Public Works and the regulations issued for their execution by the Administration.

TITLE IV.

OFFENSES OF OWNERS OF CONCESSIONS AND LESSORS OF RAILROADS.

ART. 12. The owner of the concession or the lessor for the operation of a railroad who shall not comply with the general document of conditions, or the special ones of the concession, or the resolutions for the execution of these clauses in everything referring to the operation of the line, or of the telegraph, or as to navigation, or use of all roads or free course of waters, shall incur a fine of 250 to 2,500 pesetas.

ART. 13. The owner of the concessions, or the lessor, shall also be obliged to make amends for the errors and damages caused within the time fixed; if he does not do so the administration shall do it, demanding from him the amount of the expenses and attaching the earnings of the stations.

ART. 14. The owners of the concession, or lessors of the railroads, shall be responsible to the State and to individuals for damages caused by the Managers, Directors, and other employees in the service and operation of the railroad and telegraph. If the railroad is operated by the State, the State shall be subject to the same liability in regard to individuals. Let it be understood that what has been stated in this article is without prejudice to the personal liability which Managers, Administrators, Engineers, and all classes of employees may incur, and the discretionary authority which in cases of strikes, disturbances of public order, and conspiracies appertains to the Government.

ART. 15. The Department of Public Works, without intervening in the appointment of the employees of the companies for the service of operating the railroad, may require the company to dismiss the employees whom it may consider dangerous to the safety of passengers and the maintenance of public order.

TITLE V.

TRANSGRESSIONS AND CRIMES AGAINST THE SAFETY AND PRESERVATION OF RAILROADS.

ART. 16. Any one willfully destroying or damaging a railroad or placing obstacles on it which shall obstruct the free transit or cause the derailing of a train, shall be punished with imprisonment. In case the train has been derailed the imprisonment shall be in the penitentiary.

ART. 17. In case the destruction or damage is caused in time of rebellion or sedition, and the authors of the crime do not appear, the principal authors or leaders of the sedition or rebellion shall incur the penalty imposed in the previous article.

ART. 18. The provisions of the preceding articles shall be understood to be without prejudice to the civil and criminal liability which the guilty parties may incur, for crimes of homicide, wounds, and injuries of all kinds which may occur, and for those of rebellion and sedition.

ART. 19. When two or more penalties concur, the Judges and Courts shall impose the greater in its maximum degree.

ART. 20. Those who threaten the commission of a crime included in Articles 16 and 17 shall be punished with the penalties provided for in Article 107 of the Penal Code. The scale therein established shall be observed, but always imposing the maximum degree, and, when the degree shall be fixed, the next highest one in its minimum degree.

ART. 21. Whosoever through ignorance, imprudence, or by reason of negligence or failure to comply with the Laws and Regulations, causes in the Railroad or its dependencies some damage which may injure persons or property, shall be punished, according to Article 581 of the Penal Code, by reason of gross negligence.

ART. 22. The engineers, conductors, brakemen, station masters, telegraph operators, and other employees charged with the service and care of the line, who abandon their respective posts while on duty, shall be punished with the same penalties. But if some injury is occasioned to persons or things, they shall be punished with the penalty of correctional imprisonment or minor imprisonment.

ART. 23. Those who interfere with the railroad employees, while performing their duty, shall be punished with the penalties which the Penal Code imposes on those who resist the agents of the Government.

ART. 24. Those who violate the Regulations included in Titles 1 and 2 of this law, the Regulations of the Administration, and the orders of the Governors as to police, safety, and operation of Railroads, shall be punished with a fine of 15 to 150 pesetas, according to the gravity and circumstances of the case and its perpetrator. If, according to the Penal Code, they have incurred a graver penalty, only the latter shall be imposed. In case of recurrence of the crime the fine shall be from 30 to 300 pesetas.

ART. 25. Those not paying the fine imposed upon them shall be liable to execution against the person, according to the provisions of Article 50 of the Penal Code.

ART. 26. Without prejudice to the penalties stated in the preceding articles, those who shall have infringed the Regulations of this Law shall destroy the excavations, constructions, and covers, take away the deposits of inflammable material, or of any other kind which may have been made, and repair the damages occasioned in the Railroads. The Mayors shall fix a time for the performance after hearing the representative of the Administration of the Railroad or the Company itself. If within the time fixed this shall not be done, the Government shall do it at the expense of the party who may have disobeyed. In this case the collection of the expenses shall be made in the same manner as that of taxes.

TITLE VI.

PROCEDURE.

ART. 27. Those who commit crimes punishable under this law shall be tried in the ordinary way, whatever be their right to other trial.

ART. 28. Those who have only incurred a fine shall be excepted from the provisions of the preceding article. For the imposition of the fines the following rules shall be observed:

1. The right to inform belongs to the people.

2. The denunciations shall be made to the Municipal Judges in whose districts the transgression was committed.

3. The proceedings and steps in these actions shall be the ones provided for in cases of common transgressions.

4. The testimony of those in charge of the management of the road and the sworn guards shall be sufficient, except when there is evidence to the contrary.

5. Municipal Judges shall see to the fulfillment of the penalties imposed in these cases.

ART. 29. The penalties imposed on the owners of the concessions or lessors of the railroad in the cases mentioned in Article 12 may only be imposed by the Governors after hearing the interested parties, the Chief

Engineer of the Division, and the Council of Administration which hears disputes. The fines imposed by the Governors on the owners of concessions or lessors of railroads shall not be remitted except by the Department of Public Works, after hearing the Council of State.

Therefore: We command all Tribunals, Justices, Chiefs, Governors, and all other authorities, civil, military and ecclesiastical, of any class and dignity whatsoever, to observe and to see that the present law is observed, carried out, and executed in all its parts.

Given at the Palace on the 23d of November, 1877.

I, THE KING.

C. FRANCISCO QUEIPO DE LLANO,
            Secretary of Public Works.

REGULATIONS FOR THE EXECUTION OF THE RAILROAD LAW OF NOVEMBER 23, 1877.

CHAPTER I.

ARTICLE 1. The lines of general service, constituting the plan of this class of works, having been fixed by Article 4 of the Law of Railroads, in order to make any change in the said plan the formalities expressed in the said law and the provisions of these Regulations must be complied with.

ART. 2. Whenever it may be deemed necessary or convenient to add a railroad line to the plan, a preliminary plan of the same must be made, in conformity with the provisions for such cases of Article 9 of the Regulations of July 6, 1877, for carrying out the General Law of Public Works.

This preliminary plan shall consist of the following documents:

1. An explanatory memorial, in which a general description of the works shall be made, and the convenience of the line and the utility of the railroad, the construction of which is to be of general interest, shall be shown.

2. A general plan and a longitudinal profile, which shall show the direction to be followed by the line and shall demonstrate the possibility of its realization within the technical conditions acceptable in this class of roads.

3. An estimate, as near as possible, of the cost of the railroad, including the rolling stock necessary for its operation.

4. The principal items of the schedule of fares and freights which are to be adopted for the operation of the work; and

5. Statistical data as to the probable business of the road which it is proposed to construct, so as to be able to judge of the advantages to be derived from its construction.

The preliminary plans shall be drawn subject to the existing instructions or those ordered for the purpose by the General Direction of Public Works, Commerce, and Mines.

ART. 3. When the initiative to include a line in the plan comes from the Government, the Secretary of Public Works shall order that the preliminary project to which the preceding article refers be drawn by the Engineer or a Board of Road, Canal, and Port Engineers, which may be for the purpose designated, the General Direction of Public Works, Commerce, and Mines issuing the special instructions which may be considered proper.

The said initiative may come also from a Municipal Council, Provincial Deputation, or any other official corporation, and also from individuals or companies who are interested in the construction of the line, as provided for in Article 28 of the Law. In this case the interested corporations or individuals shall present to the Department of Public Works a petition accompanied by the preliminary plan and the documents referred to in the preceding article.

In all cases where the declaration of general service is asked for, the petition shall be published in the Gazette and official Bulletins of the proper Provinces, granting a month for the presentation of petitions by other private corporations or companies which may ask the same declaration in their favor. Those wishing to make use of this right shall present their petition within the time fixed, accompanying it with the proper preliminary plan, in order that the proceedings provided for by Article 29 may be followed.

ART. 4. The preliminary plan or plans admitted shall be submitted in the report provided for by Article 28 of the Law, to which these Regulations refer, and the tenth of the Regulations for the construction of Public Works.

After this formality has been complied with the papers shall pass to the Consulting Board of Roads, Canals, and Ports for report as to the technical part of the work, as well as to the propriety of the declaration of general service and as to which of the petitions should be preferred.

ART. 5. In view of the results of the proceedings mentioned in the preceding articles, the Secretary of Public Works shall decide as to the propriety of the declaration requested and as to the preliminary plan which should be preferred. If the decision be in the negative, the matter shall be considered ended without further action, returning the preliminary plan or plans, as the case may be, to the corporations or individuals who may have presented them. If the decision be favorable, the Secretary of Public Works shall present to the Cortes the proper form of Law, accompanied by all the documents relative to the report and the preliminary plan which shall have deserved the preference.

The law having been promulgated, the line shall be declared of general service, being included in the general plan of railroads of this class, and considered as of public utility for the purposes of the law of eminent domain, all in conformity with Articles 5, 6, and 7 of the Special Law of Railroads.

ART. 6. When the declaration of general service shall be asked for in favor of a line devoted to the operation of coal or iron veins, the proceedings indicated in Articles 2 to 5 of the present Regulations shall be followed; but to the report, referred to in Article 4, shall be added another of an expert, in which the engineers of the branch and the Superior Expert Board shall be heard as to the importance of said mineral veins, as provided for in Article 8 of the Law.

A similar procedure shall always be followed when it is a question of projected branches or important industrial centers, hearing in these cases the Deputations and the Boards of Agriculture of the interested Provinces and the Council of Agriculture, Industry, and Commerce.

CHAPTER II.

CONSTRUCTION OF RAILROADS BY THE STATE.

ART. 7. Whenever the Government shall consider it necessary or proper to proceed with the construction of a railroad declared of general service, with State funds, and by administrative methods or by the usual contract, the Secretary of Public Works shall appoint an Engineer, or a Board of Road, Canal, and Port Engineers, who shall make the proper plans according to the provisions of Article 57 of the Railroad Law.

The Engineer or Board appointed for the purpose shall, above all, make an estimate of the expenses occasioned by the plans, according to Article 4 of the Regulations for the execution of the Law of Public Works, complying with what is prescribed in said article as to the approval of the estimate.

ART. 8. The documents which shall constitute all railroad plans which the Government may order drawn shall be those stated in Article 6 of the Regulations for the execution of the General Law of Public Works, and shall be drafted according to the following provisions:

1. The memorial shall include the description of the line and of the works of greater importance, the number, class, and situations of the stations, and a plan of the laying out of the lines and levels, with a statement of the curves of the lines.

2. A general plan and longitudinal profile of the line, as well as the plans and profiles by sections, and in case of buildings included in the project there shall be added all the necessary details and notes to give a complete idea of the plan.

3. In the document of conditions a description of the works shall be made, and the requisites shall be stated which the materials employed in said work must have, as well as everything relating to manual labor and employment in the works.

4. The estimate shall contain the details of cubic measurement, the prices of the work to be done, and other facts necessary to show the total cost of the railroad.

All these documents shall be drawn according to the forms used for drafting railroad plans, or according to those provided for in the future, as well as those general rules of the service and special instructions which the General Direction of Public Works, Commerce, and Mines may deem it proper to order.

ART. 9. To the said documents mentioned in the previous article, which are those constituting the plan in its technical part, the following shall be added:

1. A detailed statement of the material which may be necessary for the construction and operation of the railroad.

2. A detailed schedule of the maximum passenger and freight rates, with instructions giving the proper rules for the application of the schedule.

3. Statistical facts as to the probable business of the proposed railroad, calculating, in view of such facts and the application of the schedule, what profits shall accrue from the construction of the work.

For drafting these documents the existing provisions, or those ordered in the future for the purpose by the proper General Direction, shall be taken into account.

The plan shall also be accompanied by the document of special and economic conditions referred to in No. 3 of Article 17 of the Regulations of the 6th of July, 1877, and should contain all the provisions therein stated.

ART. 10. In case the province or towns interested in the construction of a railroad shall oblige themselves to help the State, sharing with it the cost of construction, there shall be added to the papers the memoranda in which the obligations contracted by the said corporations shall be formally stated, with the specifications of the aid offered and the time when it shall be paid to the Government.

ART. 11. The Secretary of Public Works may submit for the report of the Corporations which he may deem competent the plan and documents referred to in the previous articles, but on condition of always hearing the Consulting Board of Roads, Canals, and Ports.

These formalities being complied with, the plan may be approved by the Government.

ART. 12. The plan of a railroad having been approved, the proper form of law shall be presented to the Cortes, asking authorization for the construction of the line, as provided for in Article 10 of the Law of November 23, 1877. Said legislative authorization having been obtained and funds having been appropriated for the purpose, the construction of the line shall be proceeded with according to the plan and the technical economic conditions annexed to it, and according to the provisions of Articles 14 to 17 of the Regulations for the execution of the General Law of Public Works, the towns and provinces interested, in the proper case, being obliged to pay the State the aid which they may have offered.

ART. 13. The construction of a line being finished, it shall be determined by the Government if the operation of a railroad shall be by the State or by contract, in view of the provisions for such cases of Article 27 of the General Law of Public Works of April 13, 1877, and 53 of the Law of November 23, of the same year. If the work is to be by contract, the contractor shall receive the earnings according to the schedules approved for the use and operation of the railroad, during the time which shall be stipulated, and shall deliver every year to the State a sum as compensation for the expenses incurred in the construction of the line.

The contracts shall always be made by public bids, which shall refer to the most advantageous annual payment to be made, as provided for in the last paragraph.

ART. 14. For the lease of the operation of a railroad constructed by the State, the proper document of conditions shall be carried out which shall be approved by the Secretary of Public Works, after hearing the Consulting Board of Roads, Canals, and Ports.

In the said document there shall be stated:

1. The annual sum to be paid by the contractor, which is to serve as the basis for the bids;

2. The number of years during which the contractor is to enjoy the receipts of the earnings fixed in the schedule;

3. The rolling stock which is to be used in the operation, whenever it is stipulated that the stock is to be paid for by the contractor and not by the State;

4. That the maintenance and repair of the works of all kinds and of the rolling stock shall be at the expense of the contractor during the term of the contract;

5. That the contractor is bound not to interrupt the service unless by reason of force majeure, and to deliver the road in good condition for service at the expiration of the contract, a similar declaration, if deemed proper, being made as to the rolling stock;

6. The causes for rescission of the contract, and the consequences of that rescission; and

7. All the other provisions considered proper, as provided for in such cases by Article 54 of the Regulations of the 6th of July, for the execution of the General Law of Public Works and in Article 28 of the same Regulations in cases of concession.

CHAPTER III.

CONSTRUCTION AND OPERATION OF RAILROADS BY CONCESSIONS TO INDIVIDUALS OR COMPANIES WITHOUT SUBSIDY OR AID OF PUBLIC FUNDS.

ART. 15. The lines of general service, the plans of which may have been studied by the Government, may be constructed by granting concessions to individuals or companies, in conformity with the provisions of the General Law of Public Works and Chapters 2 and 3 of the

Regulations for its execution, according to whether the lines be constructed without any aid whatsoever, or with the subsidies mentioned in the law of railroads of November 23, 1877.

In the construction of a railroad by concession, the general conditions fixed or which may in the future be fixed shall govern, as well as the technical conditions forming part of the plan and the special and economic conditions which may be stipulated in each case. Those conditions undetermined in the general ones, shall be made special; also the schedule rates, the dates on which the work is to begin and end, the amount of bond to be given, and the other special clauses which may be determined on for the granting of the concession.

ART. 16. The study of a line declared of general service may be made by individuals or companies, provided these shall petition and obtain the superior authorization which is required for that purpose by Article 58 of the Law of November 23, 1877.

The authorization shall be granted with the formalities stated in Article 59 of the same Law, and in 21 of the Regulations of the General Law of Public Works.

The plans which may be presented by individuals shall consist of the same documents, and be drafted in the same form, as those mentioned in Articles 8 and 9 of the present Regulations for Railroads constructed on account of the State.

ART. 17. The individuals or companies who ask for a concession of a line declared of general service, without subsidy, shall present to the Secretary of Public Works a petition, accompanied by the complete plan of the road, drawn according to the provisions of the previous article, and by the document showing that the deposit of one per cent of the amount of the estimate has been made. The plan being presented, the petition shall be published in the *Gaceta de Madrid* and in the official Bulletins of the interested Provinces, granting a time of thirty days, which can not be extended, for the admission of other petitions for concessions which may be better than the one presented, according to the provisions of Article 64 of the General Law of Public Works.

ART. 18. If the time fixed in the previous article has elapsed, and no other new plan has been submitted, that of the petitioner shall be sent to the Engineer in Chief of the proper Division, so that he may compare it on the ground and report as to the plan of the line. The expense of the comparison shall be borne by the petitioner, who must deposit the amount in the Provincial Treasury, as is provided for in Article 24 of the Regulations for the execution of the General Law of Public Works.

After the project has been returned by the Engineer in Chief, it shall be submitted for the report provided for in Article 24, and afterwards passed to the Consulting Board of Roads, Canals, and Ports, whose opinion shall not only refer to the technical part of the plan but also to the examination of the proposed schedules and other circumstances, which are to be taken into consideration in granting the concession, as stated in Article 26 of said Regulations.

ART. 19. If, after all the steps are taken, it be necessary or advisable to modify the plan, either in its technical or economic part, or in the conditions under which the concession is to be made, it shall be returned to the petitioner for him to make the proper corrections within the time fixed for the purpose, or for him to withdraw his petition if it be not convenient for him to modify his plan.

When the interested party shall not be satisfied with what is finally decided by the Government as to the points in controversy, the plan shall be considered abandoned, and shall be returned to the petitioner, together with the deposit which may have been made.

ART. 20. In the case to which the preceding articles refer, namely, when it is a question of a petition for a concession without subsidy, and for which only one proposition shall have been presented, said concession shall be granted without the formalities of public auction; but always by means of a Law, as provided for in Article 27 of the Law of Railroads.

To this end the Secretary of Public Works shall present to the Cortes the proper form of Law, accompanied by all the documents mentioned in Article 25 of the Law of November 23, 1877, and in the corresponding articles of these Regulations.

ART. 21. The law to which the preceding article refers being passed, and the bond of 3 per cent of the amount of the estimate being deposited within the time fixed by Article 16 of the Law of Railroads, there shall be issued to the interested party, or to the company which may have solicited the concession, the proper instrument, making the contract a public document, and including in it, verbatim, the document of general conditions, the special law of concession, the special and economic conditions, and schedule of maximum rates.

During the number of years fixed by the law of concession, which shall not exceed ninety-nine, the owner of the concession may operate the road and enjoy the privileges and exemptions mentioned in Chapter IV of the Law of Railroads, as well as the right to seize by eminent domain, according to existing provisions, the lands and buildings necessary for the construction of the work.

ART. 22. The owner of the concession shall proceed in the construction of the work according to the conditions of the concession, and under the inspection which appertains to the Government agents, as determined by the General Law of Public Works and Article 40 of the Regulations of July 6, 1877.

During the construction no changes or modifications may be introduced which shall not have been duly authorized, after reports of the Engineers in charge of the inspection and supervision of the works and the opinion of the Consulting Board of Roads, Canals, and Ports.

The bond of 3 per cent shall not be returned to the owner of the concession until he shall show that he has work completed of a value equivalent to a third of the amount of that embraced by the concession, as provided for in Article 17 of the Law of November 23, 1877.

ART. 23. The work being all concluded, the owner of the concession shall make, at his own expense, with the assistance of the Government Engineers, the survey and detailed plan of the railroad and all its appurtenances, drawing also a descriptive plan of the stations, bridges, buildings, and constructions which may have been made.

Of each of the documents and plans mentioned in the preceding paragraph, and of the notes of the survey, a copy properly legalized shall be delivered by the owner of the concession to the General Direction of Public Works during the first year of the operation of the line or section of the line to which they refer.

ART. 24. A railroad, or part of it, shall not be placed in operation without the authorization of the Secretary of Public Works, after report on the examination of the work and construction material, drafted by the Government Engineers charged with the inspection, and in which it shall be declared that the railroad may be open to the public. Said report shall be sent to the Government by the Governor of the proper Province, with his own report.

ART. 25. The companies owning concessions shall operate the railroads during the years fixed by their concessions in conformity with the approved schedule and according to the conditions which may have been stipulated for its application.

The said companies shall draft the necessary Regulations for the good service, administration, and operation of their lines, submitting the Regulations to the approval of the Secretary of Public Works when they affect the safety of the operation or the relations of the public to the companies.

The owners of the concessions are at liberty to choose, without any other restrictions than those imposed by existing provisions, the personnel of all classes for the construction and operation of the lines, as well as the organization of this personnel, and everything pertaining to the internal government of the companies.

The Secretary of Public Works shall exercise through his agents the inspection and supervision which belongs to him by law, not only as to the expert, but also as to the administrative supervision, the companies owning concessions complying with the orders which the said agents shall communicate to them within the scope of their authority and according to the provisions in such cases.

ART. 26. The companies shall be obliged to keep in good condition the railroad and its appurtenances, so that travel may be constant, easy, and safe. All the expenses for maintenance and repairs, ordinary as well as extraordinary, shall be defrayed by the companies.

The railroads shall be considered and cared for like other public roads, and the trackmen who shall be named by the companies owning concessions may use the same arms and enjoy the same privileges as the road repairers (*peones camineros*) of the highways of the State. In order that the said trackmen may be entitled to claim these privileges, they must wear the badge agreed on by the companies, which they are to use while performing their duties.

ART. 27. Whenever the Government may consider it proper to revise the schedule in conformity with the right which is given it by Article 49 of the Law, it shall proceed, whatever may be the change intended, to an investigation, in which there must be heard without fail the company owning the concession, or the Board of Agriculture, Manufactures, and Commerce of the Provinces traversed by the Railroad, or the Deputations of the same, the Engineer in Chief of the Division, the Governors, the Consulting Board of Roads, and the Superior Council of Agriculture.

After the investigation has been concluded there shall be ordered, in a proper case, by means of a Royal Decree the reduction to be made in the schedules; and, if the company owning the concession does not consent to the reduction, the Secretary of Public Works shall submit to the Cortes the proper form of Law to carry the reduction into effect, and to determine the means for guaranteeing to the owner of the concession, the earnings of the year preceding the revision and the progressive increase of the receipts, which the railroad may have had in the five years which terminated with said year.

ART. 28. Besides the cases of forfeiture provided for in Article 36 of the Railroad Law, there shall be also those determined by the Special Law of concession, and by Article 61 of the General Law of Public Works.

ART. 29. For the purposes of Article 36 of the Law, the following shall be considered cases of force majeure:

1. Floods or rising of rivers whenever they are greater than those that by tradition, or in any other trustworthy manner, are known to have occurred in more or less distant epochs.

2. Fires occasioned by the electricity of the atmosphere.

3. Epidemics.

4. Earthquakes.

5. The sinking of the earth and landslides, where the work is constructed or to be constructed, as well as the breaking off of great blocks or masses of mountains, or extraordinary snowslides.

6. The destruction caused in time of war by belligerent forces or those occasioned by sedition of the people.

7. Robbery by mobs and violent destruction. And

8. In general those extraordinary accidents, the effects of which are evidently irresistible.

ART. 30. Whenever the owner of a concession shall ask for an extension to finish the works of his concession, based on damages produced by an unforeseen accident, he shall address himself to the Secretary of Public Works within the period of twenty days, which can not be extended, counted from the date of the occurrence, stating the damages which have occurred or injuries occasioned, the causes to which they may be attributed, the means employed to avoid the damages, and the time which, in his judgment, shall be required for the repairs.

After hearing the Chief Engineer of the Division to which the line belongs and the Railroad Section of the Consulting Council, the Secretary of Public Works shall draft an interrogatory, so that it shall serve as a basis for the investigation to be made of the fact.

In this investigation the Provincial Deputations, the Municipal Councils of towns in which the damage may have occurred, the Chief Engineers of the same Province and that of the proper Railroad Division shall be heard.

The proper Governors shall direct the investigation in whatsoever refers to their Provinces, and after it has been concluded the paper shall be sent with their report to the General Direction of Public Works, Commerce, and Mines.

The said papers shall afterwards pass to the Consulting Board of Roads, Canals, and Ports, so that it may report as to the declaration of unavoidable accident and as to the petition of extension made by the owner of the concession.

The full Council of State shall finally be heard in conformity with the provisions contained in paragraph 1 of Article 36 of the Law of Railroads.

ART. 31. The provisions of the preceding article having been complied with, the Secretary of Public Works may extend the time fixed in the Law of Concessions, bearing in mind the provisions of said Article 36 of the Law.

Similar proceedings shall be instituted when the owner of the concession shall desire to avoid forfeiture because of the total or partial interruption in the operation of the railroad by reason of unavoidable accident or of force majeure; the request in such case shall be passed upon by the Secretary of Public Works.

ART. 32. The proceedings for forfeiture of a concession may be commenced by the Secretary of Public Works on his own initiative, or by virtue of an appeal of the Chief Engineer of the Division, the Deputation, the Board of Agriculture, Manufactures, and Commerce of any of the interested Provinces, or the Governors of the same.

The official or corporation which may consider that there is a case of forfeiture, shall address the Secretary of Public Works in a memorial, giving the reason on which the appeal is based. This petition shall be passed to the owner of the concession, so that he may answer the charges, and afterwards, on this basis, an investigation shall be made by the Governors of the interested Provinces in which the authorities and corporations mentioned in the first paragraph of the present article shall be heard, and, lastly, said authorities shall submit the result of their investigation to the Secretary of Public Works.

The papers shall again be passed to the owner of the concession, fixing a time, which can not exceed thirty days, for him to state whatever he may consider best in his defense, after which the Consulting Board of Roads, Canals, and Ports, and the full Council of State shall be heard.

In view of the report, if it be proper, the forfeiture shall be declared by the Secretary of Public Works. The owner of the concession may appeal from this decision, according to the provisions of Article 34 of the Law of Railroads.

ART. 33. The consequences of the delaration of forfeiture of a railroad line shall be those specified in Articles 37 to 41, inclusive, of the Law of Railroads.

When a concession is finally declared forfeited, in order that the said provisions shall take effect, the Engineers of the State appointed by the Secretary of Public Works and the experts appointed by the concessionaire shall proceed to the contradictory survey and valuation of the work constructed in the line, the material collected for the same, the rolling stock devoted to its operation, as well as all kinds of buildings and appurtenances. The survey and valuation shall be adjusted to the rates of the estimate which accompanied the plan of the road, and a memorial explaining the operations made shall be added, stating the condition of the work and material at the time the appraisal is made, and the real value, if they have suffered any damage by reason of age or wear, or by defects of construction, as well as the plans of the road, and of all kinds of buildings and work. Should any difference of opinion about the appraisal exist between the State Engineers and the representatives of the company, each part shall make a separate report, stating the facts about which there is any difference and the grounds thereof.

The opinion of the Consulting Board of Roads, Canals, and Ports shall be heard afterwards, as to the survey and valuation, and as to the claims of the interested party, in the proper case.

ART. 34. The valuation of the works and materials, made in conformity with the provisions of the preceding article, and duly approved afterwards by the Secretary of Public Works, shall serve as the basis for the application of Articles 37 to 41 of the Law.

From the final amount of the appraisal, the bond, or part of it, returned, at the time of the declaration of forfeiture, to the owner of the concession, shall be deducted, according to Article 69 of the General Law of Public Works, and Article 35 of the Special Law of Railroads. The expenses of the appraisal shall also be deducted, and the remainder shall be the basis for the auction referred to in the articles mentioned of the said general law.

ART. 35. At the expiration of the time of the concession the Government shall take the place of the company owning the concession, with all the rights of property to the lands and work mentioned in the said statement or plan, referred to in Article 23 of these Regulations, and shall immediately enter into possession of the railroad, together with all its appurtenances and earnings.

The company shall be obliged to deliver, in good condition for service, the railroad and its appurtenances, such as stations, wharves, stores, at the starting and terminal points, guard and watch houses, offices, etc.

It shall also be obliged to deliver, in good condition for service, the rolling stock in the minimum amount determined by the special conditions of the concession.

ART. 36. Two years before the legal termination of the concession the Secretary of Public Works shall appoint an Engineer or a Commission of Engineers to make the general examination of the line and of all its dependencies, as well as of the rolling stock of all kinds and other material which the owner of the concession is to deliver to the State, according to the preceding article. The Secretary of Public Works shall be immediately advised of this examination and in view thereof shall order whatever is necessary, so that the work, building materials, and other appurtenances shall be in good condition on the day when the owner of the concession is to make the delivery. If the owner of the concession refuses to obey the orders communicated to him, the Secretary of Public Works shall order their execution at the expense of the company, even if for that purpose it shall be necessary to attach the earnings of the railroad.

ART. 37. On the day of the expiration of a concession, the company owning the concession shall make formal delivery of the road, its material and appurtenances, according to the stipulated condition, to whomsoever the Secretary of Public Works shall appoint, with a detailed inventory, and according to the special instructions in the premises. A memorandum of the delivery shall be drafted and signed by the representative of the Secretary of Public Works and the concessionaire. The document shall be forwarded to the Secretary of Public Works, without whose approval the delivery shall not be considered valid. Said approval shall only be given after hearing the Consulting Board of Roads, Canals, and Ports.

ART. 38. The memorandum of delivery being approved, the road, with all its appurtenances and material, shall pass into full possession of the State, its operation being carried on at the expense of the State and under the Secretary of Public Works.

If the Government should decide that the operation is to be made by contract, the provisions of Articles 13 and 14 of these Regulations shall be followed, the company whose concession has terminated being preferred on equal conditions, if the said company shall see fit to make use of the right conferred upon it by this article.

ART. 39. If, within the time fixed in Article 17 of the present Regulations, one or more petitions for concessions have been submitted, an examination on the ground stated in Article 18 shall be made of each plan admitted, as well as the investigation provided for in Article 24 of the Regulations of the General Law of Public Works. This investigation shall be enlarged so as to compare the plans submitted, in order to ascertain if any one deserves the preference.

The Consulting Board of Roads, Canals, and Ports, and the Department of the Interior of the Council of State, shall then make a report thereon of the preference to be given to one of the plans in competition, being determined by a Royal Decree, so as to grant the concession requested to its author, and to return the plans as well as the corresponding deposits to the individuals or corporations which presented the same.

The proper Law having been promulgated, according to the provisions of Article 20 of these Regulations, the subscriber of the accepted proposal shall be declared the owner of the concession, after he has made the deposit of the bond of 3 per cent of the estimate, within fifteen days, counting from the date in which the order granting the right is communicated to him.

ART. 40. If it be found from the investigations, in the opinion of the Secretary of Public Works, that among the best propositions of petition for the concession of a railroad line, there is an equality of conditions in two or more of the said propositions, the concessions shall be made after the bidding at a public auction, in which the first plan presented shall serve as a basis, provided its author shall be satisfied with the changes he may have had to make according to the provisions of Article 19 of these Regulations.

If he should fail to agree, the plan which is to serve as a basis for the auction shall be designated, according to the provisions for such cases of Article 34 of the Regulations of the General Law of Public Works.

ART. 41. The plan which is to serve as a basis for the bidding being determined, and before presenting to the Cortes the form of Law of the concession, an appraisal of the plan shall be made, complying in all respects with the provisions of Article 35 of the Regulations for the execution of the General Law of Public Works.

This formality being complied with and the law of concession being promulgated, the auction shall be advertised for three months. At the auction not only the subscribers to the proposals presented and admitted may participate, but all those who may desire to do so and show a certificate of having deposited 1 per cent of the amount of the estimate made.

The proceedings to be followed at the auction shall be the same as those provided for in Articles 36, 37, and 38 of the Regulations of the General Law of Public Works, the concession being declared granted to the bidder offering the best terms, with the understanding that the subscriber of the plan which has served as a basis for the auction is to have the right to collect from the auction sale the value of the said plan.

ART. 42. The concession being approved, the owner of the concession shall deposit within fifteen days from the date on which the decision of the auction shall be communicated to him the bond of 3 per cent of the amount of the estimate which served as a basis for the auction. To this end the proper communication shall be personally delivered to him; a receipt shall be exacted, in which the date of its delivery shall be stated.

In case the author of the plan which has served as a basis for the auction should not be the owner of the concession, he shall prove by a trustworthy document, within a month from the date mentioned in the preceding paragraph, that he has paid the author of the said plan the amount of the appraisal to which paragraph 1 of the preceding article of these Regulations refers.

ART. 43. The party obtaining the concession of a railroad line in any of the cases and terms provided for in Articles 39 and 41 of these Regulations shall have the obligations and shall enjoy the rights which are stated in the existing Laws for concession of works without subsidies, and, finally, in the construction of the works and in the operation of the railroad there shall be observed, as to the concession, the provisions of Articles 22 to 37 of these Regulations.

CHAPTER IV.

CONSTRUCTION AND OPERATION OF A RAILROAD BY CONCESSION TO INDIVIDUALS OR COMPANIES SUBSIDIZED WITH PUBLIC FUNDS.

ART. 44. When the Government itself shall have made the plans of a railroad line in the terms provided for in Articles 7 to 9 of these Regulations, and shall deem it proper to have it constructed by concession, granting a subsidy in any of the forms stated in Article 12 of the Law of Railroads, a hearing shall be had as to the plan and as to the necessity of a subsidy and its nature and amount, the Provincial Deputations, the Boards of Agriculture of the interested Provinces, and the Governors being heard. The Consulting Board shall report, and after this formality is complied with, and in view of the result of the hearing, the Secretary of Public Works shall submit to the Cortes the proper form of Law, in which there shall be stated the clauses of the concession, the schedule according to which it shall be operated, the number of years which the concession is to last, the aid to be given to the owner of the concession, the form and time of paying the subsidy, and the other requisites provided for by the Laws and Regulations.

In the same form of Law there shall be fixed the proportion and form in which, together with the State, the province and towns interested in the line are to contribute to the subsidy granted, according to the provisions of Article 13 of the Law of Railroads.

ART. 45. The law of concession being sanctioned and promulgated, the line shall be offered at auction within a period of three months.

The public sale shall be held according to the existing instructions, and in order to take part in it the bidders must deposit beforehand, at the place designated by the advertisement, a sum equal to 1 per cent of the amount of the estimate approved.

The subsidy fixed shall serve as a basis for the auction, and the object of the proposals shall be the reduction of the said subsidy.

ART. 46. If the subsidy consists of the delivery to the company of certain works constructed at the expense of the State and according to the provisions of Articles 7 to 12 of these Regulations, the bidding shall be first on the reduction of the schedules, the auction being held according to paragraph 3 of Article 36 of the Regulations of the General Law of Public Works.

If there be two or more of the most advantageous propositions apparently equal, new bids shall be required, as provided for in Article 37 of said Regulations; and if none of the interested parties make any proposition whatsoever in this new bidding, he who shall have obtained the lowest number in the drawing by lot, which shall have preceded the opening of the proposals in the first bid, shall be declared the best bidder.

The record of the auction being made and it being approved by the Secretary of Public Works, he who shall appear as the best bidder in the first or second bids referred to in the previous articles shall be declared the owner of the concession.

ART. 47. If the subsidy consists of the delivery to the company of a part of the invested capital, which part is to be fixed exactly in the law of concession, the auction shall be first on the reduction of the amount of the subsidy, and afterwards, in case of equality of proposals, on the reduction of the schedules; and if there still be equality of proposals, on the number of years of the concession, all in strict accordance with the provisions for such cases of Articles 43 and 44 of the Regulations of the General Laws of Public Works.

ART. 48. In the third and fourth cases of Article 12 of the Law of Railroads, namely, when the subsidy consists in granting the constructor of the line the right to take advantage of other works constructed for public use, compatible with the use of the railroads, or in the exemption of the duties on material of construction or operation, the auction shall be, in the first place, on the reduction of the schedules, and then on the reduction of the number of years of the concession, proceeding in all matters according to the provisions of Article 46 of these Regulations.

ART. 49. The owner of the concession shall deliver at the proper place and at the time fixed in Article 16 of the Law of Railroads a bond equivalent to 5 per cent of the estimate approved; the said amount shall not be returned until all the works included in the concession shall have been entirely finished. The bond being given, the construction of the works shall be proceeded with according to the clauses and conditions of the concession.

ART. 50. If the subsidy consists of works already constructed by the Government, they shall be delivered to the owner of the concession after making an inventory and appraisal of them, which shall be inserted in the proper record, the owner of the concession signing the receipt therefor.

If the aid consists of the delivery of a sum in specie or bonds and stocks, it shall be paid to the company in the form and time stipulated, always on a certificate of the Engineers of the State charged with the inspection. The payment of the subsidies in these cases shall be made to the company by the Government directly, and the Government in its turn shall be paid by the provinces and the towns the part of the subsidy devolving upon them, as determined by the Law.

When any public work compatible with the use of the railroad is to be delivered to the company owning the concession, the delivery shall be made with the formalities stated in the first paragraph of this article.

If the subsidy consists of the exemption of customs duties, the formalities determined in the existing provisions or those provided in the future by the proper Law or Regulations shall be complied with.

ART. 51. The concession of a railroad, to which a subsidy has been granted, shall be forfeited in the cases provided for by the General Law of Public Works and by the Law of Railroads.

Exception shall be made in the cases of force majeure, set forth in Article 29 of these Regulations, which must be proven in accordance with Article 49 of the General Law of Public Works.

In case of forfeiture, from the appraisal which must be made in accordance with the provisions of Articles 33 and 34 of these Regulations, there shall be deducted the amount of the bond, if it should have been returned, the expenses of the appraisement and auction, and the lands, works, money, or other things of value which may have been delivered to the owner of the concession. The remainder shall be the amount for which the completed works and the materials on hand shall be sold at auction.

The provisions of the Law and the corresponding articles of these Regulations shall be followed in all other proceedings for the purpose of declaration of forfeiture and its consequences.

ART. 52. In the execution of the work the owner of the concession shall confine himself to the approved plan, in which no variations or modifications may be introduced, without the proceedings specified in Article 22 of these Regulations. In such case the consequences of the variations authorized shall be those designated in Article 19 of the Railroad Law.

In the execution of the work and in the operation of a subsidized line, the provisions of Articles 23 to 27 of these Regulations shall be observed concerning the plans and documents which must be made on the completion of the work, the necessity of authorization to begin the operation of the road, the privileges and obligations of the owner of the concession in its operation, and the formalities necessary for a revision of a schedule of rates.

In like manner the provisions of Articles 35, 36, and 37 concerning the formalities with which the railroad shall be delivered at the termination of the concession shall be observed.

ART. 53. When an individual, or a company, desires the concession of a railroad with a subsidy, he shall direct the proper petition to the Secretary of Public Works, accompanying the plan, in accordance with Articles 8 and 9, and proving that the deposit of 1 per cent of the estimate has been made.

In the petition there shall appear the kind of subsidy prayed for, stating its amount and the form in which it shall be made, with a full argument, in order to prove the necessity or desirability of the aid which is asked for.

ART. 54. When the documents referred to in the preceding article have been received, there shall be published in the *Gaceta de Madrid* and in the official bulletins of the interested Provinces the proper advertisements, fixing a period of thirty days for the admission of proposals which might be more advantageous than the first.

If the time fixed should pass and no proposal whatever be made, or if those presented should not be admissible, because of the absence of certain of the requirements of the Law or of these Regulations, the plans shall be forwarded to the Chief Engineer of the proper Division, in order that he may actually go over the ground and make the report referred to in Article 18.

Thereon the proceedings provided for by Article 44 shall be instituted, and as a result of the same the approval of the superior authorities may be given to the plan and other documents.

In case that it should be deemed necessary to introduce any modifications in the plan or in any of the clauses of the concession, the provisions made for such cases by Article 19 of these Regulations shall be observed.

ART. 55. When the plan is approved and when the basis of the concession is agreed upon, the appraisal of the studies shall be made, which shall be done in accordance with Article 35 of the Regulations for the execution of the General Law of Public Works.

ART. 56. The Secretary of Public Works shall present to the Cortes the proper form of Law in order that the construction of the railroad may be authorized.

The said proposed Law shall be accompanied by the plan approved for the line in question with all the other documents necessary to determine the basis of the concession, the schedule of rates, the kind and form of the subsidy which the State shall give, the part which shall be contributed by the interested Provinces or Municipalities, and the other requisites which are demanded by the Laws and Regulations.

When the Law is promulgated, the concession shall be offered at auction during a period of three months, as provided for by Article 45 of these Regulations; in such case it must be stated that the author of the plan proposed has a right to the concession on the same terms as the highest bidder, and also that otherwise he shall be paid by the person to whom the concession is granted the expenses of his plan, in accordance with the appraisal made, in relation to which the provisions of Article 42 of the Regulations for the execution of the General Law of Public Works shall be observed.

The proceedings, rules, and prescriptions contained in Articles 46 to 52 of these Regulations, referring to the case in which the petition for the construction should have emanated from the Government, are applicable in all respects to the case in hand; that is, to the construction by means of a concession of a subsidized railroad on the request of an individual or company.

ART. 57. If within the time fixed by Article 54 admissible proposals should have been presented for the construction of a railroad, the provisions of the same, concerning going over the plans on the ground and the proceedings which must be had thereunder, shall be extended to them and to the corresponding plans. The Engineer in Chief as well as those reporting shall make the comparison in their decisions of the various plans presented, giving their opinion concerning the order of preference in which they should be considered.

Thereafter the opinion of the Consulting Board of Roads, Canals, and Ports, and of the Department of Public Works of the Council of State, shall be taken concerning all matters involved in the proceedings, and as a result of all this the Secretary of Public Works shall decide which plan should be selected; then proceeding to its appraisal in the manner provided for in analogous cases by these Regulations.

The other plans shall be returned to the authors with the deposits they made on presenting them.

ART. 58. In case the first plan and any other of those thereafter presented should be equally favorable, the first shall have preference and its project shall be the one appraised and shall serve as the basis of the concession.

When two or more of the proposals made after the first shall be equal, the one which was first presented shall have the preference, and its project shall be the one appraised and shall serve as the basis of the concession.

The provisions of Article 23 of the Regulations for the execution of the General Law of Public Works shall be strictly observed in such cases, to prevent all doubt concerning the date of the presentation of such plans.

ART. 59. When the plan which is to serve as a basis for the concession, determined by either of the means indicated in the two preceding articles, according to the circumstances, shall have been appraised, the proper form of Law shall be presented to the Cortes, and concerning the auction or auctions, construction or operation, and delivery of the road, in cases where there is a subsidy, the provisions of Articles 45 to 52 of these Regulations shall be observed.

CHAPTER V.

INSPECTION AND SURVEILLANCE OF RAILROADS.

ART. 60. The direction regarding the construction, operation, and police supervision of the railroads appertains to the Secretary of Public Works, as well as the surveillance which he shall exercise over them, in accordance with Articles 60 and 61 of the Railroad Law, and they shall take their course in compliance with the special instructions which now govern or which may hereafter be adopted, in accordance with the principles laid down in these Regulations.

ART. 61. The inspection which the Government should exercise over railroads is divided into technical or expert and administrative or business inspection. Both classes of inspection shall be conducted by officers under the authority of the Secretary of Public Works, who may order that the personnel of whatever kind assigned to the inspection shall depend on the Chief Engineer of the Division, or that the expert and administrative inspections shall be made by officials independent of each other.

ART. 62. The expenses of the inspection shall be defrayed by the State or by the railroad companies, according to the stipulations in the clauses of the concession of each line.

In case the companies should be obliged to pay all or part of the above-mentioned expenses the payment shall be made directly by the State. The sums which for this purpose are paid by the companies should be credited to the proper items of the appropriation.

ART. 63. The expert inspection shall also be considered divided into two parts, namely, first, that which should be made of the construction, line and works, and technical operation; and, second, that which should be made of the material and traction.

Everything referring to the study, comparison and examination of the plans, to the construction of the lines, preservation and repair of the work, roadway, fixed material and buildings, to the surveillance of the line, of the signals and switches, and to the makeup and velocity of the trains, shall be considered as appertaining to the first division.

The second division shall include everything in connection with the preservation and repair of the rolling stock.

ART. 64. The expert inspection shall be made by Engineers of the Board of Roads, Canals, and Ports, aided by mechanical engineers, when the Government may deem it proper, by assistants from among the subordinate employees of Public Works, and by watchmen who fulfill the requirements of these Regulations.

Art. 65. The expert inspection shall be made in each of the Divisions created, or to be created in the future, by a Chief Engineer in charge of the employees mentioned in the previous article, in case this service should be separated from the management. The mechanical engineers serving in the Divisions, shall be especially in charge of the preservation and repair of the rolling stock, discharging their duties under the orders of the Engineers of the proper Divisions.

Art. 66. The expert officers who make the technical inspection shall be appointed by the Secretary of Public Works in the same manner as those serving in the Department of Public Works. Mechanical engineers shall be appointed in like manner. Watchmen serving under the expert inspectors shall be appointed from the list of retired soldiers who may have served in expert corps or in the civil guards (*guardia civil*), provided they receive recommendations for good behavior in their discharge papers.

Employees of this class shall not be removed from the service, except for malfeasance or misfeasance committed therein, after proceedings instituted in accordance with the rules established for that purpose.

Art. 67. All that concerns the business operation, the relations between the public and employees of the company engaged in that branch, to the jurisdiction and supervision which the Government should exercise over these employees, and the safety of travel, in case of attempt to wreck the trains, or in case of public disturbances, is under the charge of the administrative inspection of railroads.

Art. 68. The employees of the Administrative Inspection shall consist of Chief Inspectors, Special Inspectors, and Commissaries, whose number and salaries shall be fixed in the appropriation bills, in accordance with the necessities of the service.

Art. 69. The employees connected with the Administrative Inspection shall be appointed by the Secretary of Public Works in accordance with the present provisions, or with those that shall in the future be adopted, of the Laws and Special Instructions in this connection.

Said employees shall have accurate knowledge of the General Laws of Railroads, of their conditions and schedules of rates under the Law, and the police Regulations of the same, and such directions as may have been issued by the Government and by the companies concerning the telegraph service and the business operations of the lines.

Art. 70. Inspectors and Assistant Inspectors in charge of the administrative inspection of railroads can not be removed except through malfeasance and misfeasance in office, and after the proper proceedings in accordance with the rules established for this purpose.

Chapter VI.

RAILROADS DEVOTED TO PRIVATE USE.

Art. 71. Railroads devoted to the service of an industry or to private use, for the construction of which the use of public lands is not required nor condemnation proceedings desired, may be built without any other formality than a notification to the Superior Civil authority of the proper Province, and may be thereafter operated without any other restrictions than those imposed by the Health Laws and Laws for the Public Safety, in the manner determined by Article 62 of the Railroad Law.

Art. 72. When an individual or company desires to build a railroad line for the service of a private industry, and needs for that purpose the use of public lands, the interested party shall present to the Secretary of Public Works a petition accompanied by the proper plan.

This plan shall only be in the nature of a memorial explaining it and a description of the route, a general plan and a general profile, the particulars of the public lands traversed by the line, the plans and grades of the construction proposed for said lands, and the approximate estimate of the cost of these works.

Art. 73. The papers mentioned in the preceding article shall be sent to the Governor of the proper Province, who shall open the investigation concerning these works as prescribed by Article 67 of the Railroad Law. The Governor shall hear in this proceeding the Municipal Councils of the towns traversed by the line, the Provincial Deputation, and the Chief Engineer of the Province. Said official shall then send the papers, with his report, to the Secretary of Public Works, who, by means of a Royal Decree, may grant the authority asked for after hearing the Consulting Board of Roads, Canals, and Ports.

When the authority is granted, the petitioner may construct and operate the road without other restrictions than those imposed by the public health and public security and the conditions which may have been imposed in the order granting the authority for the use of public property which may have been issued.

Before beginning the work the interested party shall give security equivalent to 5 per cent of the estimated cost of the work to be constructed on public lands, which security shall be returned to him when he proves that he has fulfilled his obligations.

Art. 74. The part taken by the administrative agents in the concessions referred to in the two preceding articles shall be limited to seeing that the exact conditions imposed for the building of the work to be undertaken on public lands granted to the owner of the concession are fulfilled.

Authorizations of this kind shall be revoked if the owner of the concession should not absolutely fulfill the stipulations of the order granting the concession; in such case the work done on the public lands shall be destroyed and all material removed, in order that such lands may be clear and in the same condition as they were before the granting of the concession.

The owner of the concession may appeal in an action against the Royal Decree of revocation, but when the latter is affirmed he shall lose the security given, and the lands granted shall again be public property.

ART. 75. For the construction of all railroads devoted to public service, although not of general interest, and for the construction of all those which, although devoted to a private industry or to private use, may be used by the public, the use of the public domain may be asked for, and also the right of condemnation of private lands, as provided in Article 64 of the Railroad Law.

In such cases the company, individual, or interested party shall direct to the Secretary of Public Works a petition, accompanied by a plan of the line, in accordance with the provisions of Articles 8 and 9 of these Regulations.

The documents constituting the plan shall be annexed to those which the petitioner considers pert.nent to prove the necessity of condemnation and to a list showing the municipal districts of the property owners whose estates should be occupied.

ART. 76. The Secretary of Public Works shall send to the Governor of the proper Province the plan and documents mentioned in the preceding article, so that he may institute the investigation prescribed by law. This investigation shall treat simultaneously of the consideration of the occupation of public property and of the desirability of the declaration of public utility.

The Governor shall announce the petition in the *Boletin Oficial*, with a list of the names of those interested in the condemnation, and shall order the petitioner to re-mark the ground, and shall also hear the claims presented before the proper Mayor (*Alcalde*) by the property owners or their representatives, in accordance with Article 156 of the Regulations for the execution of the General Law of Public Works.

The papers shall then go to the petitioner, in order that he may know and answer the claims presented, and the Governor, after hearing the Executive Commission of the Provincial Deputations and the Chief Engineer of the Division, shall forward the proceedings, with his own report, to the Secretary of Public Works.

ART. 77. The Secretary of Public Works shall send the proceedings to the Consulting Board of Roads, Canals, and Ports for report on the technical part of the plan, as well as on the claims and objections that may have arisen, and in order that the basis may be fixed in accordance with which the concession may be granted.

The Secretary of Public Works, with all these antecedents, shall present to the Cortes the proper form of Law, in accordance with Articles 64 and 68 of the Railroad Law.

After the Law is sanctioned and promulgated, the concession shall be granted, and, therefore, subject, ipso facto, to all that may be applicable to the provisions of Chapter III of these Regulations, concerning concessions without subsidy.

CHAPTER VII.

FORMALITIES REQUIRED FOR THE CONCESSION OF TRAMWAYS.

ART. 78. No tramway or railroad established on a public highway may be constructed without its proper plan being made and approved beforehand.

This plan shall consist of—

1. A memorial giving a description of the tramway and showing the advantages which would redound to the public interest by its construction.

2. A general plan, showing clearly the direction of the route, a general profile showing its grades, and the corresponding detailed plan, giving a clear idea of the system proposed to be used on the public highway in the various conditions in which it may be. If towns are traversed, or the tramway be established on the streets of the town, plans on a large scale shall be made of the streets traversed by the line, and its position and relation to the sidewalks and house fronts.

3. The technical conditions in which the works are described and details relative to construction are given.

4. An estimate.

5. And the schedule of rates to be charged in the operation of the tramway, with a calculation of the probable earnings of the company.

ART. 79. The approval of the plan referred to in the preceding article is the attribute of the Secretary of Public Works:—

1. When the proposed tramway shall occupy a State highroad.

2. When it shall occupy a Provincial highroad.

3. When it shall occupy in part a State highroad.

4. When it shall occupy in part a State highroad and in part a Municipal road or street.

5. When it shall occupy both a Provincial highroad and a Municipal road or street.

6. When the motive power shall be other than that of draft animals, whatever may be the kind of public road it may occupy.

ART. 80. The approval of the plan of tramways is the attribute of the Governor of the Provinces when their entire length traverses Municipal roads or streets.

ART. 81. Whenever an individual or company may desire to build a tramway of those designated in Article 79, he shall address his petition to the Secretary of Public Works, accompanied by the plan referred to in Article 78, proving that he has deposited an amount equivalent to one per cent of the estimated cost.

Thereafter the petition shall be advertised in the *Gaceta* and *Boletin Oficial* of the proper Province, fixing one month for the admission of petitions which may be better than the first.

ART. 82. If within the time fixed by the preceding article no other plan may have been submitted, that presented shall go to the Chief Engineer of the Province, so that he may go over the plan on the ground of such part as shall occupy a State highroad.

Thereafter it shall go to the Deputation, through the Governor, in order that the expert Chief of Provincial Works may also go over the plan on the ground as to that part of the tramway which shall occupy Provincial highroads.

And lastly, the Governor shall send the plan to the proper Municipal Council or Councils, so that the proper experts may go over it on the ground as to such part of the work which may occupy Municipal roads or streets within each Municipal District.

The Chief Engineer and the Chief Experts of Provincial and Municipal Public Works, who shall have gone over the plan on the ground, shall state whether the data presented is correct, and at the same time shall report on the technical parts, stating whether, in their opinion, the plan as presented may be accepted, or if there should be a necessity of introducing any modifications.

ART. 83. When, within the period of thirty days, designated in Article 81, there shall have been presented and admitted new plans, these shall likewise go to the Engineers of the State and Provincial and Municipal Expert Chiefs at the same time as the first plan, in order that all may be gone over on the ground in the manner determined by the preceding article.

In such case the report of the Expert Chiefs shall extend to the comparison of the various projects, stating whether anyone deserves the preference, and the reason therefor.

In all cases the expenses of going over the plans on the ground shall be paid by the petitioner or petitioners who submitted the respective plans.

ART. 84. The reports mentioned in the two preceding articles shall be directed to the Governor with the plans they refer to, and when these have been received by said authority he shall order that an investigation be made, as determined in such cases by the General Law of Public Works, the Regulations for carrying it into effect, and Article 87 of these Regulations.

ART. 85. When a tramway which is to occupy a State highroad only is in question, the Chief Engineer of the Province and the Executive Commission of the Provincial Deputation shall be heard in this investigation, and the Governor shall send the proceedings, with his report, to the Secretary of Public Works.

ART. 86. When only Provincial highroads are to be occupied, the Provincial Deputation shall be consulted, which shall make its report after hearing the expert Director of the Corporation; thereafter the Chief Engineer shall make his report, and, lastly, the Governor shall make his, on sending the proceedings to his superiors.

When the works are to occupy both State and Provincial highroads, similar proceedings shall be followed, adding the report of the Executive Commission, which shall be heard, after the Chief Engineer.

ART. 87. The Municipal Councils of the towns interested shall first be heard, if the tramway shall occupy in part a State highroad and in part a Municipal road or street. A public investigation shall be held in said towns for a period of at least twenty days, at which all the residents who may consider themselves interested may take part, stating what they may deem proper. The Municipal Councils, after having first consulted the opinion of the expert Chiefs, shall report. Thereupon the petitioner shall be heard, in order that he may answer the claims which may have been presented. Thereafter the Chief Engineer of the Province shall be consulted and also the Executive Commission of the Provincial Deputation; and the Governor shall be the last to report on sending the proceedings to the Secretary of Public Works.

ART. 88. Whenever both a Provincial highroad and a Municipal road or street are to be occupied, the interested Municipal Council or Councils shall first be heard, as provided for by the preceding article, and then the Provincial Deputation, which shall report after first hearing the opinion of its expert Director. The proceedings shall then go to the petitioner in order that he may answer the objections and claims which may have been made; and after this formality is complied with, the Chief Engineer and the Executive Commission shall report their opinions referring to the legal questions which might have arisen, and lastly, the Governor, who shall send the proceedings to the Government.

ART. 89. When a road in which the motive power shall be steam or compressed air, or any other than animal power, the investigations referred to in Articles 84 to 88 shall take place according to the specific case in compliance with the rules established therefor, embracing in such case the advantages or disadvantages which the motive power proposed may have, and to the conditions which, in a proper case, should be imposed to prevent the damages which might result therefrom to public travel.

ART. 90. When the plans proposed are two or more in number the investigations shall cover all of them simultaneously, and individuals, officials, and corporations giving information shall state their opinion as to which deserves the preference. In such case the petitioners shall be heard in the investigation in the inverse order of the presentation of their plans, so that the author of the first one presented shall be the last one heard, care being taken by the Governors to fix the shortest possible time for the petitioners to send their replies, with the object of shortening the proceedings.

ART. 91. In all the cases referred to in the preceding articles, after the proceedings have been received by the Department of Public Works, they shall go to the Consulting Board of Roads, Canals, and Ports for its report concerning the technical part of the plan or plans proposed, as well as the preference which shall be given to one of them, at the same time proposing the conditions in compliance with which, in a proper case, the concession may be granted.

The Secretary of Public Works shall approve the plan presented in view of the proceedings, if this shall be proper, or the one meriting the preference among those accepted.

If from the proceedings there should result that to approve the plan it should be necessary to introduce some modifications, in such case the provisions of Article 19 of the present Regulations shall be observed.

ART. 92. When the plan of tramway shall come within the provisions mentioned in Article 73 of the Railroad Law, that is to say, when the works are to occupy a State highroad and a Provincial highroad, and finally both State highroads and Municipal roads or streets after approval of the plan in the manner prescribed by the preceding article, its appraisal shall be made as is provided for analogous cases by these Regulations.

ART. 93. The Secretary of Public Works who has the power to grant the concession, in the cases specified in Article 73 of the Law, shall immediately advertise the auction of the works, for the period of two months, on the basis of the approved plan.

The auction shall take place in accordance with the provisions of Article 76 of said Law, respecting the schedules of rates, the equality of propositions as to the duration of the concession, and with the understanding that in all cases the right of legal preference shall be reserved at the auction to the author of the approved plan, and if the latter should not take advantage of the preference the successful bidder shall pay him, within one month, the value of the plan, in accordance with the appraisal made.

ART. 94. If from the investigations to be made there should appear an equality of conditions of two or more of the accepted plans, the one first presented shall have the preference, and in this case it shall be appraised and shall serve as the basis for the auction prescribed by the preceding articles.

ART. 95. When the auction is decided the declared owner of the concession shall give, within a period of fifteen days, security equivalent to 5 per cent of the estimated cost, as provided for by the law for subsidized railroads. The owner of the concession shall build the works in accordance with the stipulations and under the inspection and surveillance of the State Engineers in such parts as are occupied by State highroads. In such part as the tramway occupies Provincial highroads the inspection shall be carried on by the expert Directors of Provincial Works, and in such part as the works occupy Municipal roads or streets within towns the inspection shall be carried on by the expert agents of the Municipality.

ART. 96. When the concession expires, the term of which can not be for longer than sixty years, according to Article 76 of the Railroad Law, the Government, the Province, or the towns shall enter into the enjoyment and use of the part of the tramway built in State, Province, or Municipal roads or streets, respectively, in accordance with the special rules laid down in each case, in order to carry out the operation and sharing of the earnings among the interested parties.

ART. 97. The plans and grant of tramway concessions, in which the motive power is other than animal, shall be subject to the same proceedings as those designated in the preceding articles, in which case the Secretary of Public Works may always approve the plans and permit the individuals or companies who request it to construct these roads.

ART. 98. In tramway concessions, made by the Secretary of Public Works in the manner determined by the Railroad Law, all the provisions contained in Chapter IV of these Regulations concerning concessions of subsidized railroads, shall apply in so far as they are practicable and do not conflict with the provisions of the preceding articles.

ART. 99. If the tramway is to occupy one or more provincial highroads, after the approval of the plan by the Secretary of Public Works, in compliance with Article 91, it shall go to the Governor, in order that he may transmit it to the Provincial Deputation, which has the right to grant the concession in such case, as provided for by Article 74 of the Law.

The same shall be observed in the case of the occupation of both Provincial and Municipal roads or streets, when the Secretary of Public Works shall have the power to approve the plan, and the Deputations the power to grant the concession.

ART. 100. The Deputation shall immediately have the approved plan appraised, and shall then advertise the auction, proceeding in all other matters in accordance with the provisions of these Regulations and of the articles which may be applicable of Chapter V of the Regulations of July 6, 1877, which treats of the concessions of the construction of Provincial works.

ART. 101. If the tramway is to occupy Municipal roads or streets only, the petitioner shall send his plan, accompanied by a petition, to the Governor of the Province, who in this case has the right of approval, as provided for by Article 71 of the Railroad Law. The Governor shall order the publication in the *Boletín Oficial* of the proper advertisement, fixing a period of thirty days within which to present proposals which might better the first.

ART. 102. The plan shall then be sent to the Mayor, who shall order it gone over on the ground by the expert Chief of Municipal Works, then submitting said plan to a public investigation, directed by the said Mayor, and at which the residents of the town who deem it proper to make objections and claims shall be heard, for which purpose a time, not less than twenty days, shall be fixed.

The Mayor shall then send the result of the public investigation to the petitioner so that he may reply; then the full Municipal Council shall be heard, and with his report he shall finally send the proceedings to the Governor.

If, within the period of the thirty days mentioned in Article 101, new plans should have been presented and accepted, going over the plans on the ground, the expert report, the public investigations, and the puplic opinions of the Municipal Council and the Mayor shall embrace all the plans admitted, and also concerning the preference which, as a result of the comparison of their respective advantages or disadvantages, one deserves over all the others competing.

ART. 103. The Governor, on the opinion of the Provincial Chief Engineer, shall decide the approval of the plan. When he considers the work of great importance, or when he disagrees with the opinion of the Chief Engineer, he shall send the proceedings with his own report to the Secretary of Public Works, who shall finally decide after hearing the Consulting Board of Roads, Canals, and Ports, as provided for in Article 93 of the Regulations for the execution of the General Law of Public Works.

ART. 104. If the tramway is to occupy Municipal highroads or streets within a single Municipal District, in which case the Municipal Councils have the right to grant concessions in accordance with Article 74 of the Law, the Governor shall send the approved plan to the proper Municipal Council, which, after an appraisal of said plan, shall advertise the auction and grant the concession in accordance with the provisions of Chapter VII of the Regulations of the 6th of July for the execution of the General Law of Public Works.

ART. 105. If the tramway is to occupy roads or streets belonging to more than one Municipality, but within one Province, the plan must be separately submitted to each of the Municipal Districts it traverses, and in each of the towns the study of the plans on the ground and the investigations referred to in Article 102 of these Regulations shall be made.

The Governor of the Province, as soon as he has gathered the proceedings of the interested Municipalities, shall proceed to the approval of the complete plan in the manner provided for by Article 103.

ART. 106. After the approval of the plan by the Governor in the case stated in the preceding article, the proceedings shall go to the Provincial Deputation, which in such case has the right to grant the concession, as provided for by Article 74 of the Railroad Law.

ART. 107. When the Municipal highroads which the tramway is to occupy belong to Municipalities of different Provinces, the investigation and the other proceedings shall be carried out in each one of the Municipalities, as provided for by Article 105, and the Governors shall have to come to an agreement in all points before proceeding to the approval of the plan.

If this agreement is reached, the plan shall be considered approved and the concession shall be granted by the Deputations of the respective Provinces.

Should the Governors differ as to the approval of the plan, the matter shall be decided by the Secretary of Public Works, to whom the proceedings shall be forwarded by the said authorities. The Secretary shall finally decide after hearing the Consulting Board of Roads, Canals, and Ports.

In case there is not an agreement in all points regarding all clauses and conditions between the Deputations interested, the question of granting the concession shall be decided in the same manner. The Deputation in all other matters shall follow the provisions of Articles 99 and 100 of these Regulations.

ART. 108. Concessions of tramways made by Municipalities by virtue of the Law of Railroads and of the corresponding articles of these Regulations shall be subject, in so far as applicable and not in contradiction with what is herein provided, to the provisions of Chapter VII of the Regulations for the execution of the General Law of Public Works.

CHAPTER VIII.

GENERAL CONDITIONS WHICH SHOULD BE OBSERVED IN THE CONSTRUCTION AND OPERATION OF TRAMWAYS.

ART. 109. The Government, hearing the Consulting Board of Roads, Canals, and Ports, shall draw a set of general conditions, which shall be observed in tramway concessions, complying with the provisions prescribed in the following articles of the present Regulations.

ART. 110. Every concession of this kind shall be understood to be made without prejudice to third persons, and protecting private rights according to the provisions of Article 28 of the Regulations for the execution of the General Law.

ART. 111. The security which shall be required from the owners of concessions shall be 5 per cent of the value of the estimated cost of the approved plan, and shall not be returned until all the works included in the concession have been finished.

ART. 112. Tramways must always be established in such manner as not to cause injury nor to impede the travel of the ordinary vehicles which pass over the highroads or the streets which they occupy. In consequence, no system shall be admitted in which the rails project above the level of the road, and in the general conditions there shall be determined the minimum width of the streets in which the tramway may be constructed, fixing the position which the rails must occupy, in order that the tram cars may cross ordinary vehicles in movement and those stopping in the highway or in the street, loading and unloading. Thus, also, proper rules shall be established in order that travelers on foot may not suffer damages or inconveniences in the road.

ART. 113. That part of the highroad or street occupied by a tramway, or that part of the width which shall be determined, shall be kept in repair at the expense of the owner of the concession, who for this purpose shall renovate and replace the bed and the pavement with material of good quality whenever this may be necessary in the judgment of the expert agents charged with the inspection.

In the construction of the tramway, and in the preservation and repair, care shall be taken to introduce no modification whatsoever, either in the grade of the highroad or streets or in the transverse profile affected by them.

ART. 114. When the tramway is to be of a single track, turnouts conveniently situated shall be built, in order to avoid any blockade.

ART. 115. The works must be carried out in accordance with the approved plan, in which no modification whatsoever may be introduced without the approval of the Secretary of Public Works, or, in a proper case, of the Governor of the Province.

ART. 116. No tramway shall be placed at the disposal of the public until after inspection by the Engineers or expert agents of the Deputations or of the Municipal Councils, according to the circumstances. These officials shall report the result of their inspections to the Governor of the Province, and if the reports should be favorable, the Governor shall decide that the tramway be open to the public service, reporting to the Secretary of Public Works in all cases in which the concession may have been granted by that Department.

ART. 117. The company shall operate the tramway during the time stated in the concession, in accordance with the approved schedule of rates, which in no case shall be higher than those fixed therein.

The owner of the concession shall be obliged to assure the travel on his road, except in cases of force majeure. If the travel should be interrupted from causes imputable to the owner of the concession, the Department of Public Works, or the Deputation, or the Municipal Council which may have granted the concession, shall adopt the measures conducive to its reestablishment at the expense of the company.

ART. 118. The company may freely decide on the means of constructing the road as well as on the selection of the employees appointed for its operation and administration. In the same manner the necessary rules for the public service shall be drafted, notifying the Department of Public Works or the proper authority as the case may be.

In matters relating to public health and safety the company shall do what is demanded by the Government and the proper authorities, in conformity with the General Laws and Regulations and the special police laws of highroads and the Municipal ordinances of the towns through which the line passes.

ART. 119. At the expiration of the concession the company shall turn over to the proper party, in good serviceable condition, the tramway, its dependencies, material, and means of traction, and the Government, Deputations, or Municipal Councils, to whom the delivery is made, shall enter into the full enjoyment of the income earned by the operation of the tramway.

ART. 120. Besides the general conditions governing the concession of all tramways, other special conditions shall be stipulated which shall contain the provisions relating to the times in which the work should begin and end, the amount of the security, the schedule of rates allowable for the use of the works, duration of the concession, and cases of forfeiture (if any special ones are added besides those provided for by the general Law of Public Works and by the Railroad Laws), with everything else deemed convenient for the good construction of the road and of interest for the public service.

ART. 121. When the motive power employed for the traction is other than animal, it shall be stipulated in the general conditions that the engines, should they be run by steam, shall not produce smoke, nor any special noise which might frighten the horses of ordinary vehicles; that powerful brakes be used in order to stop the train in the shortest possible time; that the speed shall not exceed 20 kilometers per hour on the highroads, and that it shall be moderated until equal to that of a horse at a walk while within the towns, as well as where travel may be very active; that the best system of signals be adopted; and that, in short, there shall be observed all the rules and precautions possible, in order that ordinary traffic may be carried on without impediment and without danger, as well as to avoid accidents of any kind.

In no case shall the change of animal motive power established in a tramway to a different motive power be authorized without previous permission granted by the Secretary of Public Works, in accordance with the provisions of the Law in every respect and of the corresponding articles of these Regulations.

Madrid, May 24, 1878.

Approved by His Majesty.

C. TORENO.

PUBLIC WORKS.

The Colonial Department communicates to His Excellency the Governor-General, under date of June 28 last, the following Royal Order:

YOUR EXCELLENCY: In compliance with article 27 of the Budget Law for this Island, of the 5th of this month, His Majesty the King (whom God Preserve) has deemed proper to approve the provisional decree for the concession of railroads in the same, attached hereto. This I communicate to Your Excellency by Royal Order for your information and consequent effects.

And His Excellency having ordered its compliance on the 28th of July last, it is published in the *Gaceta Oficial* for general information.
Habana, August 10, 1880.

JOAQUIN CARBONELL,
Secretary of the General Government.

PROVISIONAL DECREE FOR THE CONCESSION OF RAILROADS IN THE ISLAND OF CUBA.

ART. 1. In compliance with article 27 of the Budget Law for the Island of Cuba of June 5, 1880, the Governor-General shall grant the concession for the construction and operation of the railroad lines preferred in said law and of any other ones granted in accordance with the same.

ART. 2. The general clauses, guaranties, subsidies, and franchises with which said concessions shall be granted shall be those stated in said law and in the General Law of Railroads and Police of the same, of November 23, 1877, and their respective Regulations of May 24, 1878, and September 8, of the same year, in so far as they do not conflict with article 27 of the Budget Law of Cuba aforementioned.

ART. 3. The concessions of all the lines shall be granted by means of an auction and for the period of ninety-nine years, at the expiration of which they shall pass to the ownership of the State.

The auctions for the lines enjoying, as an advance to be refunded during the entire period of the concession, an annual subsidy for every kilometer in operation, shall be held on the amount assigned to each line as subsidy, and it shall not exceed in any case $700 for each kilometer.

54

For the lines enjoying a guaranty of interest on the principal used in the construction, said interest shall be 8 per cent per annum, and the auction shall be held on the capital earning it.

For the lines without subsidy or guaranty of interest on the capital invested, the auction shall be held on the limit of time in which they are to be constructed.

ART. 4. The Inspection of Public Works of Cuba shall draft, within the maximum period of one month, the plan of the maximum schedules to be applied to all lines which may hereafter be granted in the Island, as well as that of the provisions which are to be observed in the collection of the amounts of these schedules, which shall also be common to all the lines.

This plan of schedules and of provisions for their application shall be briefly annotated by the Consulting Board of Public Works and afterwards by the Council of Administration of the Island, and the Governor-General shall approve the same, with the modifications which he may deem proper.

Subsequent changes shall be submitted to the Government.

ART. 5. The technical conditions of the plan of the construction of the subsidized lines shall be determined by the Inspection of Public Works. In consequence thereof, in view of the studies already made of some of the lines and of the date which can be procured for the rest, it shall fix the time table for each one of them, showing the towns and principal points through or in the vicinity of which the line is to pass, the minimum radius of the curves, the maximum grade of the levels, the class of the principal works of art which are to be of a permanent character, and the limits of time to be granted to commence the works, and to place each section of the line in operation. The gauge of the line shall be the standard one in the Railroads of Cuba, but in special and duly authorized cases it may be narrower. In the stations and switches which may be established for the meeting of trains, there shall be two tracks at least.

ART. 6. The Inspection of Public Works shall also propose for each line at the same time as the conditions stated in the preceding article the maximum limit of the subsidy to be refunded which it shall enjoy during the period of the concession and annually for each kilometer in operation, if this plan of subsidy is adopted.

In case the annual subsidy is preferred, the guaranty of interest on the capital invested in the construction, the Inspection shall determine the maximum capital per kilometer which is to be recognized as having a right to said guaranty and the cost of operation which, as the limit, is to be recognized to the concessionaire in order to estimate the profit he may make; but it being understood that if the real expenses of the operation are less than the maximum cost calculated, the former shall be the ones to be considered in order to determine the net proceeds of the operation.

ART. 7. The lines which do not enjoy a subsidy in either of the two manners stated are not subject to technical conditions of drafting and construction, nor to the maximum schedules.

ART. 8. The Inspection of Public Works shall draft the conditions for the concession of subsidized lines. Those for lines which are not subsidized may be presented by the companies or individuals.

ART. 9. After the conditions of a line are drafted, they shall be submitted for the report of the Consulting Board of Public Works and by the Council of Administration of the Island, and the Governor-General may approve them, notifying the Government thereof immediately.

ART. 10. After the conditions of construction of a line have been approved by the Governor-General or by the Government, according to the cases, the public auction for the award of the concession shall be advertised.

ART. 11. The auctions shall be held at Habana, being advertised at least three months beforehand. In order to take part therein it shall be necessary to deposit 1 per cent of the capital assigned to each line for the guaranty of interest. This deposit may be increased to 3 per cent of the said capital within the period of thirty days from the date on which the award is announced and it shall serve as a guaranty for the compliance of the conditions of the concession. The guaranty shall be returned to the concessionaire when by means of a certificate of the Inspecting Engineer it is proven that an amount equal to double the value of the former has been invested in works, the guaranty being then replaced by the works executed.

ART. 12. After the concession of a line has been awarded, the inspection of the public agents shall only take place in so far as is necessary to secure the compliance of said conditions and in regard to the public safety, the operation being permitted when the line or its sections fulfill their conditions, without prejudice to said works being terminated and the rolling stock completed within reasonable limits of time.

ART. 13. The Governor-General shall report to the Government all the vicissitudes and progress which each line may encounter.

ART. 14. The Treasury of the Island shall credit to the concessionaire of the lines which enjoy an annual kilometric subsidy the amount due half yearly for the kilometers operated, the earning of the subsidy for each section commencing from the first day of the half year following the opening of each one. From this amount there shall be deducted, in accordance with law, 50 per cent of the gross proceeds earned during the half year by the section operated, and the difference shall be the amount paid to the concessionaire of each line as refundable subsidy.

When, during four consecutive half years, 50 per cent of the gross proceeds of a line exceeds or equals the subsidy, the concessionnaire shall lose all his right to a further subsidy, but the Treasury shall continue to collect the excess of the 50 per cent over the amount of the subsidy until it has recovered the payments which it may have made for this purpose in previous half years, without making any charges whatsoever of interest for the advance.

ART. 15. For lines enjoying a guaranty of interest, the latter shall be applied to the capital or to the cost per kilometer obtained at the auction, or to the number of kilometers operated in each complete half year. From the amount of the half-yearly interest thus obtained there shall be deducted the net proceeds, viz, the difference between the gross proceeds and the expense of operation, determined by the second paragraph of article 6 of this decree. The difference between the interest for the half year and the net proceeds shall be what the Treasury of the Island shall pay to the respective concessionnaires.

When during four consecutive half years the net proceeds of the operation of a line computed in the manner above mentioned equal or exceed 8 per cent per annum on the capital which is to earn the same, the right to the guaranty of interest shall cease in the future; but the Treasury shall continue to collect 50 per cent of the excess over the said 8 per cent.

ART. 16. As long as the right to the collection of the subsidy or to the guaranty of interest exists for each line, the public administration shall exercise in the economic management of the enterprise the intervention necessary to ascertain the gross proceeds of the operation as well as to assure itself that the expenses of the same are not lower than those fixed for each line. There shall be understood by operating expenses only those caused by the surveillance, preservation and repairing of the line, its works, buildings and material, those of the personnel and rolling stock, operation, workshops and warehouses, those of the general management and other similar ones; but by no means the interest and amortization of loans, the increase in works or material, and all others which do not relate to the operation of the lines.

ART. 17. The Government shall not interfere in any manner whatsoever in the management of lines constructed without subsidy.

Madrid, June 28, 1880.

Approved by His Majesty:

SANCHEZ BUSTILLO.

A true copy:

CARBONELL.

ADDITION.

[Budget Law of June 5, 1880.]

PUBLIC WORKS.

ART. 27. The Government shall facilitate the construction of the Railroad system of the Island of Cuba, preferring the following lines:
Santa Clara to Sancti Spiritus.

Sancti Spiritus to San Luís de la Enramada, via Ciego de Avila, Puerto Principe, Victoria de las Tunas, Cauto Embarcadero, Bayamo, and Jiguaní.

Victoria de las Tunas to San Luis de la Enramada, via Holguin.
Bayamo to Manzanillo.
Puerto Principe to Santa Cruz del Sur.
San Miguel de Nuevitas to Zanja.
Holguin to Gibara.
Canoa to the Bay of Nipe.
El Cristo to Guaso.
Santa Catalina de Guaso to Sagua de Tánamo.

The concessions for the different sections of these lines must be awarded at a public auction, the basis therefor being the subsidy or the capital to be guaranteed by the State, according to the case, and by means of a bond, granting as a subsidy—

1. Exemption from import duties on the necessary material.

2. An annual payment of an amount not to exceed $2,700 per kilometer operated, by way of an advance, refundable with one-half of the gross proceeds of the operation or with a guaranty of interest on all or on a part of the capital invested in the line, sharing half of the dividends in the latter case, when the shareholders earn more than 8 per cent interest.

3. The gratuitous cession to the enterprises of lands owned by the State or towns which may be necessary for the construction and operation of the lines.

4. The right of condemnation by way of public utility and after indemnification for the private property indispensable for the construction and operation.

These concessions shall enjoy the franchises mentioned in Article 4 of the General Railroad Law of November 23, 1877.

The Government is hereby authorized to grant these concessions without requiring a plan previously approved, but subject to determined technical conditions of draft and construction and to a fixed itinerary; the two General Laws of November 23, 1877, and their corresponding Regulations being understood as applicable in so far as they do not conflict with the foregoing prescriptions.

Lines may be granted without the subsidy referred to in the second case of the second paragraph, and these lines shall enjoy the other franchises and rights mentioned in this Law. They shall also be awarded at a public auction, giving a bond, and the time within which the work is to be constructed shall be the basis for the bid, being awarded to the Company offering to do the work in the shortest time.

(*Gaceta,* July 1, 1880.)

www.ingramcontent.com/pod-product-compliance
Lightning Source LLC
Chambersburg PA
CBHW022036080426
42733CB00007B/850